Kids

SUMMER

ACADEMY

ARGOPREP

7 DAYS A WEEK

12 WEEKS

Mathematics
English
Science
Reading
Writing

Fitness
Yoga
Experiments
Mazes
Puzzles

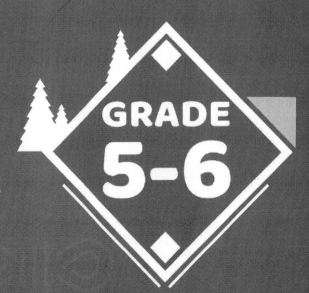

GRADE
5-6

ArgoPrep is one of the leading providers of supplemental educational products and services. We offer affordable and effective test prep solutions to educators, parents and students. Learning should be fun and easy! For that reason, most of our workbooks come with detailed video answer explanations taught by one of our fabulous instructors.

Our goal is to make your life easier, so let us know how we can help you by e-mailing us at: info@argoprep.com.

ISBN: 978-1946755728
Published by Argo Brothers, Inc.

Aknowlegments:
Icons made by Freepik, Creaticca Creative Agency, Pixel perfect, Pixel Buddha, Smashicons, Twitter, Good Ware, Smalllikeart, Nikita Golubev, monkik, DinosoftLabs, Icon Pond from www.flaticon.com

TABLE OF CONTENTS

TABLE OF CONTENTS

TABLE OF CONTENTS

TABLE OF CONTENTS

HOW TO USE THE BOOK

Welcome to **Kids Summer Academy** by ArgoPrep.

This workbook is designed to prepare students over the summer to get ready for **Grade 6**.

The curriculum has been divided into **twelve weeks** so students can complete this entire workbook over the summer.

Our workbook has been carefully designed and **crafted by licensed teachers** to give students an incredible learning experience.

Students start off the week with English activities followed by Math practice. Throughout the week, students have several fitness activities to complete. Making sure students stay active is just as important as practicing mathematics.

We introduce yoga and other basic fitness activities that any student can complete. Each week includes a science experiment which sparks creativity and allows students to visually understand the concepts. On the last day of each week, students will work on a fun puzzle.

HOW TO WATCH VIDEO EXPLANATIONS
IT IS ABSOLUTELY FREE

Step 1 - Visit our website at: www.argoprep.com/books
Step 2 - Click on the JOIN FOR FREE button located on the top right corner.
Step 3 - Choose the grade level workbook you have.
Step 4 - Sign up as a Learner, Parent or a Teacher.
Step 5 - Register using your email or social networks.
Step 6 - From your dashboard cick on FREE WORKBOOKS EXPLANATION on the left and choose the workbook you have.

You now have life time access to the video explanations for your workbook!

WHAT TO READ OVER THE SUMMER

One of the best ways to increase your reading comprehension level is to read a book for at least **20** minutes a day. We strongly encourage students to read several books throughout the summer. Below you will find a recommended summer reading list that we have compiled for students entering into Grade **6** or simply visit us at: www.argobrothers.com/summerlist

Author: Joan Aiken
Title: The Wolves of Willoughby Chase

Author: Anne Frank
Title: Anne Frank: The Diary of a Young Girl

Author: Gary Paulsen
Title: Hatchet

Author: Mark Twain
Title: The Adventures of Tom Sawyer

Author: Kevin Henkes
Title: Words of Stone

Author: Wendelin Van Draanen
Title: Flipped

Author: David Almond
Title: Skellig

Author: Gordon Korman
Title: Schooled

Author: Laurie Halse Anderson
Title: Fever

Author: Andrew Clements
Title: Things Not Seen

OTHER BOOKS BY ARGOPREP

Here are some other test prep workbooks by ArgoPrep you may be interested in. All of our workbooks come equipped with detailed video explanations to make your learning experience a breeze! Visit us at www.argoprep.com

COMMON CORE SERIES

   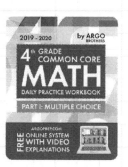

SPECIALIZED HIGH SCHOOL ADMISSIONS TEST

HIGHER LEVEL EXAMS

INTRODUCING MATH!

Introducing Math! by ArgoPrep is an award-winning series created by certified teachers to provide students with high-quality practice problems. Our workbooks include topic overviews with instruction, practice questions, answer explanations along with digital access to video explanations. Practice in confidence - with ArgoPrep!

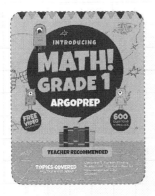   

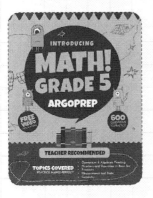   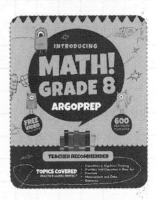

YOGA MINDFULNESS

If you are looking for a fun way to engage with your children while helping them build a mindful, engaged and healthy lifestyle, Frogyogi's Yoga Stories for Kids and Parents is the perfect book for you and your family!

KIDS SUMMER ACADEMY SERIES

ArgoPrep's **Kids Summer Academy** series helps prevent summer learning loss and gets students ready for their new school year by reinforcing core foundations in math, english and science. Our workbooks also introduce new concepts so students can get a head start and be on top of their game for the new school year!

Welcome! Meet the ArgoPrep heroes.

Are you ready to go on an incredible adventure and complete your journey with them to become a **SUPER** student?

DIPLODOCUS

WATER FIRE

MYSTICAL NINJA

GREEN POISON

FIRESTORM WARRIOR

RAPID NINJA

CAPTAIN ARGO

THUNDER WARRIOR

ADRASTOS THE SUPER WARRIOR

Give your character a name

Write down the special ability or powers your character has and how you will help your community with the powers.

Great! You are all set. To become an incredible hero, we need to strengthen our skills in **english, math** and **science**. Let's get started.

WEEK 1

Did you know our planet, Earth, is over 4.5 billion years old? The earliest evidence for life dates back over 3.5 billion years ago. It's important to learn about our planet's history and the fascinating events that have occured.

Welcome! While you work on this workbook, we will learn some interesting facts about planet Earth and its history.

OVERVIEW OF ENGLISH CONCEPTS

Action vs. Linking Verbs

As a writer, it's impossible to write a strong, impactful sentence without an understanding of **verbs**. As you've probably heard before, verbs provide the **action** in a sentence and help us **understand what is going on**. However, that statement is something of an over-simplification. There are actually two important categories of verbs: **action verbs** and **linking verbs**.

Key Terms

Action Verb: A word that communicates an action that you can **perform** or **visualize**
- **For Example:** Walk, Swim, Run, Catch, Eat, Dance, etc.
  - * Yesterday, we **walked** to the park.
  - * I **swim** at the community center pool twice every week.
  - * My uncle and I **will eat** our weight in ribs at the cookout.

Linking Verb: A word that connects (links) the subject of a sentence to descriptions or other ideas about it.

- **For Example:** Is, Seem, Appear, Look, Taste, Smell etc.
  - * That waffle **smells** delicious.
  - * He **appeared to be** having a panic attack.
  - * Flora thought something **seemed** strange about the broken window.

Here's a Hint!

If you're trying to determine whether a verb is an **action** or **linking** verb, the best strategy is to see if you could replace that word in the sentence with a form of our most basic verb: "to be." If you could replace a verb with...

- Is, Am, Are
- Was, Were, Will Be

... and the sentence still makes perfect sense without making things **less visual or clear** for the reader, then you're dealing with a **linking verb**. That's the best and easiest strategy to identify linking verbs!

For Example...
- The dogs **sniffed** around the tree with worried looks on their faces.
  - * Could you say, "The dogs **WERE** around the tree with worried looks on their faces?"
    - * **NO!** You'd be making it **harder** for the reader to visualize what is happening in the sentence. **Sniffed** is a clear **action** verb.

- The cat **looked** annoyed when the mouse escaped into its hole.
  - * Could we say, "The cat **WAS** annoyed when the mouse escaped...?"
  - **YES!** We would not be changing the meaning of the sentence or taking detail away from the reader one bit by making the change. So, **looked** is a **linking** verb.

From "A Descent into the Maelstrom"

By Edgar Allan Poe

We had now reached the summit of the loftiest crag. For some minutes the old man seemed too much exhausted to speak.

"Not long ago," said he at length, "and I could have guided you on this route as well as the youngest of my sons; but, about three years past, there happened to me an event such as never happened to mortal man—or at least such as no man ever survived to tell of—and the six hours of deadly terror which I then endured have broken me up body and soul. You suppose me a very old man—but I am not. It took less than a single day to change these hairs from a jetty black to white, to weaken my limbs, and to unstring my nerves, so that I tremble at the least exertion, and am frightened at a shadow. Do you know I can scarcely look over this little cliff without getting giddy?"

The "little cliff," upon whose edge he had so carelessly thrown himself down to rest that the weightier portion of his body hung over it, while he was only kept from falling by the tenure of his elbow on its extreme and slippery edge—this "little cliff" arose, a sheer unobstructed precipice of black shining rock, some fifteen or sixteen hundred feet from the world of crags beneath us. Nothing would have tempted me to within half a dozen yards of its brink. In truth so deeply was I excited by the perilous position of my companion, that I fell at full length upon the ground, clung to the shrubs around me, and dared not even glance upward at the sky—while I struggled in vain to divest myself of the idea that the very foundations of the mountain were in danger from the fury of the winds. It was long before I could reason myself into sufficient courage to sit up and look out into the distance.

"You must get over these fancies," said the guide, "for I have brought you here that you might have the best possible view of the scene of that event I mentioned—and to tell you the whole story with the spot just under your eye."

"We are now," he continued, in that particularizing manner which distinguished him—"we are now close upon the Norwegian coast—in the sixty-eighth degree of latitude—in the great province of Nordland—and in the dreary district of Lofoden. The mountain upon whose top we sit is Helseggen, the Cloudy. Now raise yourself up a little higher—hold on to the grass if you feel giddy—so—and look out, beyond the belt of vapor beneath us, into the sea."

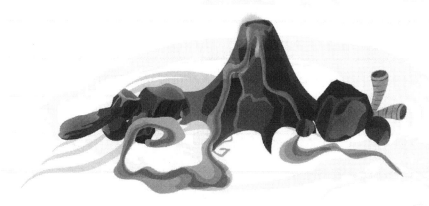

1. What kind of verb is "said," as it is used in Paragraph 2: **action or linking?** Explain how you know that answer is correct.

_____

_____

2. Why do you think the author keeps putting the phrase "little cliff" in quotation marks? What does the "little cliff" look like?

_____

_____

_____

3. What feeling does the narrator have throughout the passage?

   A. That the weather is about to get very bad
   B. That the cliffs are about to crumble
   C. That somebody bad is following him and the old man
   D. That the old man is going to betray him

4. Which of these best describes the **tone** of the passage?

   A. Uplifting
   B. Depressing
   C. Ominous
   D. Fantastical

5. Even though we don't get lengthy **descriptions** of either character in the passage, what differences can you identify between the **narrator** and the **old man?** How are their personalities, approaches, and body language distinct?

_____

_____

_____

Action or Linking Verb?

Directions: Read each sentence and then determine whether the **underlined verb** is an **action verb** or a **linking verb**. Write your answer on the line at the end of the sentence.

1. Katherine **seemed** disappointed with her grade on the science test.

   _____

   _____

2. Clark **climbed** Mount Washington over summer vacation.

   _____

   _____

3. After getting defeated by the hero at the end of the movie, the bad guy **turned** good and restored the kingdom.

   _____

   _____

4. Francesco **cooked** a delicious Thanksgiving meal for his entire family.

   _____

   _____

5. The puppet show **was** a very silly spectacle.

   _____

   _____

FITNESS

Please be aware of your environment and be safe at all times. If you cannot do an exercise, just try your best.

Repeat these **exercises 4 ROUNDS**

1 - Abs: 15 times

2 - Lunges: 4 times to each leg.
Note: Use your body weight or books as weight to do leg lunges.

3 - Plank: 20 sec.

4 - Run: 50m
Note: Run 25 meters to one side and 25 meters back to the starting position.

From "A Descent into the Maelstrom"

By Edgar Allan Poe

(Continued from Day One's Passage)

We had now been about ten minutes upon the top of Helseggen, to which we had ascended from the interior of Lofoden, so that we had caught no glimpse of the sea until it had burst upon us from the summit. As the old man spoke, I became aware of a loud and gradually increasing sound, like the moaning of a vast herd of buffaloes upon an American prairie; and at the same moment I perceived that what seamen term the chopping character of the ocean beneath us, was rapidly changing into a current which set to the eastward. Even while I gazed, this current acquired a monstrous velocity. Each moment added to its speed—to its headlong impetuosity. In five minutes the whole sea, as far as Vurrgh, was lashed into ungovernable fury; but it was between Moskoe and the coast that the main uproar held its sway. Here the vast bed of the waters, seamed and scarred into a thousand conflicting channels, burst suddenly into phrensied convulsion—heaving, boiling, hissing—gyrating in gigantic and innumerable vortices, and all whirling and plunging on to the eastward with a rapidity which water never elsewhere assumes except in precipitous descents.

In a few minutes more, there came over the scene another radical alteration. The general surface grew somewhat more smooth, and the whirlpools, one by one, disappeared, while prodigious streaks of foam became apparent where none had been seen before. These streaks, at length, spreading out to a great distance, and entering into combination, took unto themselves the gyratory motion of the subsided vortices, and seemed to form the germ of another more vast. Suddenly—very suddenly—this assumed a distinct and definite existence, in a circle of more than a mile in diameter. The edge of the whirl was represented by a broad belt of gleaming spray; but no particle of this slipped into the mouth of the terrific funnel, whose interior, as far as the eye could fathom it, was a smooth, shining, and jet-black wall of water, inclined to the horizon at an angle of some forty-five degrees, speeding dizzily round and round with a swaying and sweltering motion, and sending forth to the winds an appalling voice, half shriek, half roar, such as not even the mighty cataract of Niagara ever lifts up in its agony to Heaven.

1. What are some examples of language that the author uses to communicate that this scene is very **scary** or **traumatic** for the narrator?

   _____

   _____

2. How does this passage **escalate** (increase) in intensity as the story goes on?

   _____

   _____

3. The narrator brings up buffalo to...

   A. Provide a reference for what the hilltop smells like
   B. Provide a reference for what the jagged rocks look like
   C. Provide a reference for what the ocean sounds like
   D. Provide a reference for what kind of animals are in the area

4. What is being described in Paragraph 2?

   A. A waterfall
   B. A whirlpool
   C. A tidal wave
   D. A tornado

5. How does the author characterize **water** in this passage? What sensory details (sights, sounds, feelings) does the narrator describe that help you understand how he thinks or feels about the water?

   _____

   _____

   _____

   _____

   _____

   _____

Identify & Classify the Verb

Directions: Read each sentence and <u>underline its verb</u>. Then, on the line that follows the sentence, indicate whether it is an **action verb** or a **linking verb**. If there are **two lines** below a sentence, that means it contains **two verbs** you need to find!

1. Yesterday, Chris and I talked about the basketball game.

   _____

2. Collette appears quiet and mild-mannered at first, but she is actually very tough.

   _____   _____

3. Our family traveled to Jamaica on our last vacation.

   _____

4. Some people learn new things more quickly and easily than others.

   _____

5. Even when things look bad, you can always rely on your true friends.

   _____   _____

FITNESS

Please be aware of your environment and be safe at all times. If you cannot do an exercise, just try your best.

Repeat these
exercises
4 ROUNDS

2 - Side Bending: 10 times to each side. Note: try to touch your feet.

3 - Tree Pose: Stay as long as possible. Note: do the same with the other leg.

1 - Squats: 15 times. Note: imagine you are trying to sit on a chair.

Addition Problems

1. What is 12,265 + 248?

    A. 12,543
    B. 12,513
    C. 12,893
    D. 13,133

2. What is the sum of 4,652 and 2,358?

    A. 6,830
    B. 6,940
    C. 7,010
    D. 7,420

3. Which pair of numbers has a sum of 29,489?

    A. 14,756 and 8,983
    B. 15,768 and 14,351
    C. 24,132 and 5,547
    D. 25,814 and 3,675

4. What is 12,165 added to 12,538?

    A. 24,653
    B. 24,703
    C. 24,733
    D. 24,813

5. Which of the following number sentences is true?

    A. 43,562 + 21,275 = 64,837
    B. 23,478 + 12,935 = 35,763
    C. 56,712 + 24,532 = 80,234
    D. 34,976 + 26,534 = 61,410

6. Add 36,878 to 53,134.

    A. 89,992
    B. 90,012
    C. 90,142
    D. 90,212

7. Which number should be added to 42,865 to get the number 79,413?

    A. 36,438
    B. 36,538
    C. 36,548
    D. 37,128

8. What is 26,858 + 44,625? Show your answer.

_____

9. Write and solve an addition sentence, using these two numbers: 56,784 and 46,842

_____

10. Which of the following number sentences is FALSE?

    A. 32,725 + 3,134 = 22,625 + 13,234
    B. 26,544 + 23,627 = 33,517 + 16,554
    C. 32,943 + 25,765 = 24,765 + 33,943
    D. 54,532 + 11,684 = 61,745 + 4,471

11. What is 24,785 + 32,389 + 14,654?

_____

12. Fill in the blank to make the equation true.

25,136 + _____ + 12,678 = 50,245

13. Which pair of numbers has a sum of 59,503?

  A. 34,756 and 28,267
  B. 25,768 and 28,465
  C. 24,532 and 35,541
  D. 35,815 and 23,688

14. What is 33,165 added to 45,526?

  A. 76,651
  B. 77,731
  C. 78,691
  D. 78,811

15. Which of the following number sentences is true?

  A. 33,475 + 42,388 = 75,663
  B. 26,712 + 44,547 = 70,949
  C. 35,518 + 41,275 = 76,793
  D. 13,935 + 76,534 = 90,389

16. Add 156,856 to 123,534.

  A. 280,450
  B. 280,390
  C. 279,560
  D. 281,110

17. Which number should be added to 14,875 to get the sum 97,021?

  A. 79,986
  B. 80,126
  C. 82,146
  D. 83,116

18. What is 32,365 + 24,248?

  A. 54,543
  B. 56,613
  C. 57,193
  D. 57,433

19. What is the sum of 42,634 and 27,368?

  A. 69,982
  B. 69,992
  C. 70,002
  D. 70,012

20. Fill in the blank to make an equal problem.

34,248 + _____ + 35,382 = 113,467

FITNESS

Please be aware of your environment and be safe at all times. If you cannot do an exercise, just try your best.

Repeat these **exercises 4 ROUNDS**

2 - Lunges: 7 times to each leg.
Note: Use your body weight or books as weight to do leg lunges.

3 - Plank: 20 sec.

1 - Bend forward: 15 times. Note: try to touch your feet. Make sure to keep your back straight and if needed you can bend your knees.

4 - Abs: 15 times

Subtraction Problems

1. What is 12,598 − 8,126?

   A. 4,272
   B. 4,372
   C. 4,472
   D. 4,572

2. What is the difference between 68,325 and 29,152?

   A. 39,173
   B. 39,893
   C. 39,563
   D. 39,113

3. Choose an option in which there is an expression to get 13,671.

   A. 25,863 − 12,190
   B. 33,649 − 20,118
   C. 45,274 − 32,173
   D. 26,456 − 12,785

4. What is 84,736 − 33,167?

   A. 50,979
   B. 51,489
   C. 51,569
   D. 52,119

5. What is the difference between 34,567 and 21,175?

   A. 13,122
   B. 13,242
   C. 13,382
   D. 13,392

6. Look at this expression 76,432 − 24,868 = 51,554. Is it true? If not, write the correct answer.

   _____

7. What is the missing number in the equation 44,645 − _____ = 21,809?

8. What is the difference between 271,535 and 37,168?

   _____

9. Use subtraction to solve the following problem.

   $$\begin{array}{r} 36,948 \\ -\ 22,456 \\ \hline \end{array}$$

   _____ answer

10. Use subtraction to solve the following problem.

    $$\begin{array}{r} 65,781 \\ -\ 37,739 \\ \hline \end{array}$$

    _____ answer

11. Choose the expression that is true.

    A. 91,354 − 39,836 = 51,528
    B. 35,576 − 12,441 = 23,235
    C. 54,471 − 13,368 = 41,103
    D. 42,514 − 12,798 = 39,616

12. What is the missing number in this equation 44,176 − _____ = 23,658?

    A. 21,528
    B. 21,518
    C. 21,488
    D. 21,478

13. What is 85,376 − 37,793?

   A. 47,933
   B. 47,883
   C. 47,623
   D. 47,583

14. What is the missing number in this equation _____ − 32,497 = 26,348?

   A. 56,965
   B. 58,765
   C. 58,845
   D. 59,095

15. Which answer choice has a difference of 25,847?

   A. 51,455 and 26,478
   B. 49,351 and 15,274
   C. 63,286 and 37,439
   D. 46,307 and 21,550

16. What is 143,864 − 112,955?

   A. 30,839
   B. 30,909
   C. 31,119
   D. 31,249

17. Choose an option which is **LESS** than the difference between 85,732 and 39,864.

   A. 45,798
   B. 45,868
   C. 45,898
   D. 45,918

18. What is the difference between 45,932 and 29,574?

   A. 16,198
   B. 16,238
   C. 16,358
   D. 16,478

19. What is 96,834 − 31,727 − 12,156?

   A. 53,128
   B. 52,951
   C. 52,871
   D. 53,145

20. What is the missing number in this equation 27,301 − 12,352 − _____ = 7,356?

   A. 7,533   C. 7,593
   B. 7,693   D. 7,323

FITNESS

Please be aware of your environment and be safe at all times. If you cannot do an exercise, just try your best.

Repeat these **exercises 4 ROUNDS**

2 - Chair: 15 sec.
Note: sit on an imaginary chair, keep your back straight.

1 - High Plank: 20 sec.

3 - Waist Hooping: 15 times. Note: if you do not have a hoop, pretend you have an imaginary hoop and rotate your hips 10 times.

4 - Abs: 15 times

Multiplication Problems

1. Find the product of 5,637 and 15.

    A. 84,555
    B. 82,375
    C. 81,875
    D. 81,735

2. Choose a pair of numbers that results in a product of 10,024.

    A. 256 and 34
    B. 358 and 28
    C. 169 and 44
    D. 176 and 54

3. The number 17,758 is the result of multiplying the number 26 by _____ ?

    A. 683
    B. 648
    C. 793
    D. 813

4. What is the missing number in this equation _____ × 59 = 52,864?

    A. 656
    B. 736
    C. 896
    D. 916

5. What number multiplied by 1,247 results in the number 56,115?

    A. 35
    B. 45
    C. 55
    D. 65

6. What is 2,825 × 26?

_____

7. Determine the number that correctly fills in the blank. 539 × _____ = 19,943.

    A. 37
    B. 43
    C. 47
    D. 53

8. Solve the problem 765 × 320.

_____

9. Solve the problem:

$$\begin{array}{r} 2,648 \\ \times \quad 44 \\ \hline \end{array}$$

_____ answer

10. Which expression is true?

    A. 3,416 × 67 = 228,862
    B. 2,354 × 33 = 77,582
    C. 6,198 × 23 = 142,554
    D. 7,125 × 19 = 135,345

11. What is the missing number in the equation _____ × 27 = 36,423?

    A. 2,139
    B. 1,879
    C. 1,349
    D. 1,289

12. Find the product of 3,924 and 96.

    A. 298,964   C. 399,124
    B. 376,704   D. 278,734

13. The number 122,064 is the result of multiplying the number 48 by _____ ?

   A. 2,168   C. 2,458
   B. 2,273   D. 2,543

14. Choose a pair of numbers that results in a product of **207,680**?

   A. 64 and 3,245
   B. 56 and 3,425
   C. 62 and 3,745
   D. 58 and 3,865

15. What is the missing number in the equation $34 \times$ _____ $= 145,384$?

   A. 3,676   C. 4,276
   B. 3,956   D. 4,436

16. Which expression is true?

   A. $3,752 \times 43 = 161,436$
   B. $4,169 \times 25 = 104,225$
   C. $2,814 \times 39 = 109,736$
   D. $3,612 \times 36 = 130,132$

17. Which statement below is TRUE?

   A. $24 \times 1,278 = 30,672$
   B. $68 \times 4,372 = 294,236$
   C. $72 \times 1,563 = 112,436$
   D. $54 \times 3,071 = 214,434$

18. What is 365×125?

   _____

19. Solve the problem:

$$\begin{array}{r} 4,673 \\ \times \quad 56 \\ \hline \end{array}$$

   _____ answer

20. Find the product of 3,455 and 140.

   _____

YOGA

Please be aware of your environment and be safe at all times. If you cannot do an exercise, just try your best.

1 - Down Dog: 25 sec.

2 - Bend Down: 25 sec.

3 - Chair: 20 sec.

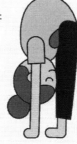

4 - Child Pose: 25 sec.

5 - Shavasana: as long as you can. Note: think of happy moments and relax your mind.

Exploring Density Using Water

We already know that objects have a **mass** or **weight** that tells us how much **matter** they are made up of, but just because two objects weigh about the same doesn't mean they have similar make-ups. Another key factor is **density**. Density is the ratio of how big something is to its mass. That means, generally, that **small things with high mass have a high density and big things with low mass have a low density.**

One great and easy way to observe density is using water. Today, we'll do a couple of quick experiments to observe how density affects the way objects interact.

Materials:

* 2 tall, clear drinking glasses
* 2 eggs, uncooked and still in their shells
* 2 small oranges, unpeeled (mandarins, clementines, etc. will all work – they just need to fit in the glasses)
* Salt
* Measuring spoons
* Notepaper
* Paper towel
* Cool running water

Procedure:

1. Fill the two cups at least two-thirds full with cool running water.

2. Look at the two oranges closely and, on your note paper, write a quick prediction of what you think will happen when you place them in the glasses of water. Do you think they will sink or float?

3. Place **one** of the oranges in one of the glasses of water. Observe what happens and write it down in your notes. Did it match your prediction?

4. Next, peel the other orange and place it in the empty glass of water. Observe what happens and write it down in your notes. The two oranges behaved differently because of **density**. The peel gives the orange a **lower** density than the water because it is filled with holes that allow the water to move through and around it. The peeled orange has a **higher** density, even though it's a little lighter, because the inner fruit is more solid and just sinks to the bottom.

5. Dump the oranges and water out of your glasses. Dry the oranges off using your paper towel and save them as a snack for later. Refill the glasses with fresh water.

6. Observe the eggs, think about what you saw with the oranges, and write down some predictions in your notes about what will happen when you place the eggs in the water.

7. <u>Gently</u> place one of the eggs into one of the glasses. Observe what happens and write it down in your notes. Did it match your prediction?

8. Using your measuring spoons, add three tablespoons of salt to the second glass of water, and stir to incorporate it well.

9. <u>Gently</u> place the second egg into the glass with the salty water. Observe what happens and write it down in your notes. The two eggs have the same density, but this time we changed the water. The regular water is less dense than the egg, which means the egg sinks. However, the salty water is more dense than the egg, which means the egg floats on top of it.

10. Carefully empty your two glasses, dry off the eggs with the paper towel, and return them to the fridge.

Follow-Up Questions:

1. Based on what you saw today, what are some other objects you already know are **less dense** than water (meaning they would float)?

_____

_____

_____

2. Based on what you saw today, what are some other objects you already know are **more dense** than water (meaning they would sink)?

_____

YOGA

Please be aware of your environment and be safe at all times. If you cannot do an exercise, just try your best.

2 - Down Dog: 25 sec.

3 - Stretching: Stay as long as possible.
Note: do on one leg then on another.

4 - Lower Plank: 12 sec.
Note: Keep your back straight and body tight.

5 -Book Pose: 15 sec.
Note: Keep your core tight. Legs should be across from your eyes.

1 - Tree Pose: Stay as long as possible.
Note: do on one leg then on another.

6 - Shavasana: 5 min.
Note: this pose is very important and provides you with long term benefits. Try not to skip this. Close your eyes and imagine who you want to be and what your goals are! Always think happy thoughts.

Task: Color in the path so the car can get to the rocket!

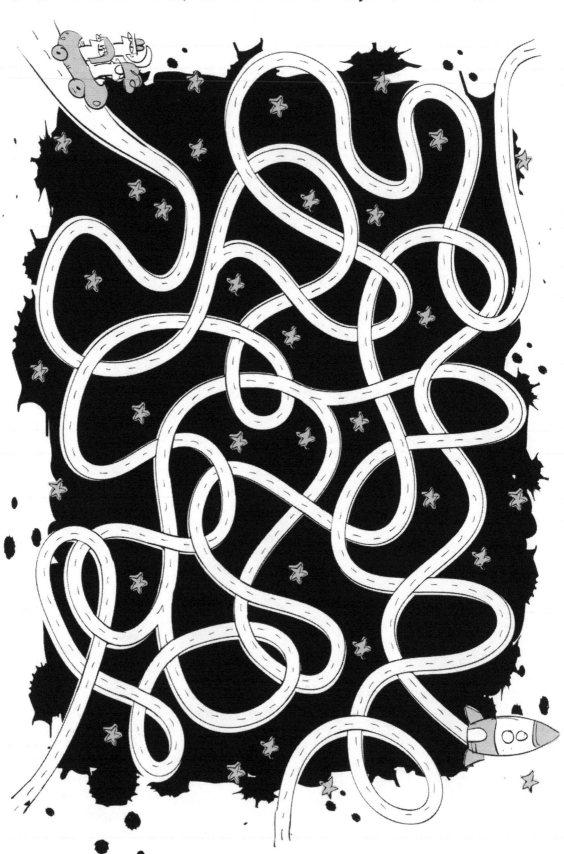

Awesome job! You have just completed Week 1. Ready to rock Week 2?

WEEK 2

Jellyfish have been around for hundreds of millions of years. These remarkable creatures have no brain or heart. In fact, they are 98% water!

Subjects & Predicates

Now that you're in middle school, you'll be reading texts with increasingly long and complex sentences. Additionally, you'll be expected to expand your own writing and use more advanced sentence structure. Before you can do that, though, you need to understand the **building blocks of sentences.** We'll start by breaking sentences down into two parts: their **subject** and their **predicate.**

Key Terms

Complete Subject: The part of the sentence that identifies the person, place, thing, or idea that the sentence is about.

Complete Predicate: The part of the sentence that contains information about what action happened or what is going on. (What did the subject do? What is the subject like?)

Hint:

- Most of the time, the **predicate** begins with the **main verb** of the sentence!
  - * It could be an **action** or **linking** verb

For Example...

In these sentences, the **complete subject** is in **bold** and the complete predicate is underlined.

- **I** went to the beach.
  - * I is the **subject.** It's who the sentence is about.
  - * ...went to the beach is the predicate because it describes what the subject did.

- **The pirate ship** fired its cannons on the Spanish galleon.
  - * **The pirate ship** is the **subject.** Notice how the **complete subject** can be more than one word. That's because, to get a full understanding of what the sentence is about, we need all of those words.
  - * ...fired its cannons on the Spanish galleon is the complete predicate because it describes what the pirate ship did (the action). We can see that it begins with the **verb**.

- **Martin and Hailey** bought twelve pieces of candy.
  - * **Martin and Hailey** is the **subject**. Notice how the **complete subject** can include more than one person or thing if those two nouns are both performing the action of the verb.
  - * ...bought twelve pieces of candy is the complete predicate because it fully describes what the subject (Martin and Hailey) did.

From "Animals of the Past"

By Frederic A. Lucas

Fossils are the remains, or even the indications, of animals and plants that have, through natural agencies, been buried in the earth and preserved for long periods of time. This may seem a rather meagre definition, but it is a difficult matter to frame one that will be at once brief, exact, and comprehensive; fossils are not necessarily the remains of extinct animals or plants, neither are they, of necessity, objects that have become petrified or turned into stone.

Bones of the Great Auk and Rytina, which are quite extinct, would hardly be considered as fossils; while the bones of many species of animals, still living, would properly come in that category, having long ago been buried by natural causes and often been changed into stone. And yet it is not essential for a specimen to have had its animal matter replaced by some mineral in order that it may be classed as a fossil, for the Siberian Mammoths, found entombed in ice, are very properly spoken of as fossils, although the flesh of at least one of these animals was so fresh that it was eaten. Likewise the mammoth tusks brought to market are termed fossil-ivory, although differing but little from the tusks of modern elephants.

Many fossils indeed merit their popular appellation of petrifactions, because they have been changed into stone by the slow removal of the animal or vegetable matter present and its replacement by some mineral, usually silica or some form of lime. But it is necessary to include 'indications of plants or animals' in the above definition because some of the best fossils may be merely impressions of plants or animals and no portion of the objects themselves, and yet, as we shall see, some of our most important information has been gathered from these same imprints.

Nearly all our knowledge of the plants that flourished in the past is based on the impressions of their leaves left on the soft mud or smooth sand that later on hardened into enduring stone. Such, too, are the trails of creeping and crawling things, casts of the burrows of worms and the many footprints of the reptiles, great and small, that crept along the shore or stalked beside the waters of the ancient seas. The creatures themselves have passed away, their massive bones even are lost, but the prints of their feet are as plain to-day as when they were first made.

1. What does Lucas mean when he writes, "This may seem a rather meagre definition, but it is a difficult matter to frame one that will be at once brief, exact, and comprehensive"?

_____

_____

2. Based on the passage, how are frozen wooly mammoths different from other fossil finds?

_____

_____

3. Based on the passage, what were "**the Great Auk**" and "**Rytina?**"

   A. Ancient plants
   B. Ancient animals
   C. Animals that were still alive when the author wrote this
   D. Animals that were recently extinct when the author wrote this

4. Which of these best describes the author's goal?

   A. To help the reader become an expert on fossils
   B. To give the reader a general understanding of what a "fossil" is
   C. To teach the reader how they can find fossils
   D. To explain to the reader how ancient animals and plants died off

5. Based on what you read in the passage, why are **not** all fossils the **same?**

_____

_____

_____

_____

_____

Identifying Subject & Predicate

Directions: Read each sentence below. Then, draw a line in the sentence that divides the **subject** from the predicate. **Remember:** The predicate usually begins with the **main verb!**

1. The quick brown fox jumped over the lazy dog.

2. My great-uncle was a fighter pilot during World War II.

3. Samantha tasted an assortment of teas from around the world.

4. The cackling mad scientist raised a glowing vial of chemicals to the light.

5. All of the members of the marching band got excused after lunch to load their instruments onto the bus.

FITNESS

Please be aware of your environment and be safe at all times. If you cannot do an exercise, just try your best.

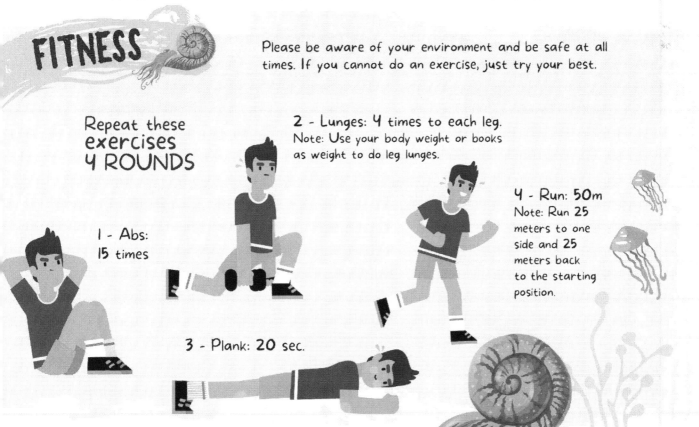

Repeat these **exercises 4 ROUNDS**

1 - Abs: 15 times

2 - Lunges: 4 times to each leg.
Note: Use your body weight or books as weight to do leg lunges.

3 - Plank: 20 sec.

4 - Run: 50m
Note: Run 25 meters to one side and 25 meters back to the starting position.

From "Animals of the Past"

By Frederic A. Lucas

(Continued from Day One's Passage)

If an animal dies on dry land, where its bones lie exposed to the summer's sun and rain and the winter's frost and snow, it does not take these destructive agencies long to reduce the bones to powder; in the rare event of a climate devoid of rain, mere changes of temperature, by producing expansion and contraction, will sooner or later cause a bone to crack and crumble.

Usually, too, the work of the elements is aided by that of animals and plants. Every one has seen a dog make way with a pretty good-sized bone, and the Hyena has still greater capabilities in that line; and ever since vertebrate life began there have been carnivorous animals of some kind to play the role of bone-destroyers. Even were there no carnivores, there were probably then, as now, rats and mice a-plenty, and few suspect the havoc small rodents may play with a bone for the grease it contains, or merely for the sake of exercising their teeth. Now and then we come upon a fossil bone, long since turned into stone, on which are the marks of the little cutting teeth of field mice, put there long, long ago, and yet looking as fresh as if made only last week. These little beasts, however, are indirect rather than direct agents in the destruction of bones by gnawing off the outer layers, and thus permitting the more ready entrance of air and water. Plants, as a rule, begin their work after an object has become partly or entirely buried in the soil, when the tiny rootlets find their way into fissures, and, expanding as they grow, act like so many little wedges to force it asunder.

Thus on dry land there is small opportunity for a bone to become a fossil; but, if a creature so perishes that its body is swept into the ocean or one of its estuaries, settles to the muddy bottom of a lake or is caught on the sandy shoals of some river, the chances are good that its bones will be preserved. They are poorest in the ocean, for unless the body drifts far out and settles down in quiet waters, the waves pound the bones to pieces with stones or scour them away with sand, while marine worms may pierce them with burrows, or echinoderms cut holes for their habitations; there are more enemies to a bone than one might imagine.

1. Why does the author mention both dogs and mice in Paragraph 2?

_____

_____

2. How do plants play a role in destroying bones and other remains?

_____

_____

3. Which of these best divides the first sentence of Paragraph 2 into its subject and predicate?

   A. Usually, too, / the work of the elements is aided by that of animals and plants.
   B. Usually, too, the work of the elements / is aided by that of animals and plants.
   C. Usually, too, the work of the elements is aided / by that of animals and plants.
   D. Usually, too, the work of the elements is aided by that of animals / and plants.

4. Based on the text, which of these places would skeletal remains best be preserved?

   A. In the ocean
   B. In the forest
   C. In a lake
   D. In the desert

5. Based on the passage, why don't we have the fossil remains of every animal that has ever lived?

_____

_____

_____

_____

_____

Confirming or Correcting Subject & Predicate

Directions: Each sentence below has been divided into its **subject** and its predicate by another student. The **subjects** should be in bold, and the <u>predicates</u> should be underlined, with a line dividing the two. Unfortunately, this student got some answers wrong!

Look at each sentence and figure out if the student has divided the sentence correctly. If they have, write "**CORRECT**" on the line below the sentence. If the sentence is not divided correctly, write "**INCORRECT**" on the line below and, using your pen or pencil, draw a new line that shows where the sentence should be divided.

1. **The elusive quarterback** <u>scrambled toward the sideline to avoid getting tackled.</u>

    _____

2. **The legendary comedy duo** <u>of Abbott and Costello made more than **35** movies together.</u>

    _____

3. **Sylvia and Becky always eat lunch** <u>on the steps of the library.</u>

    _____

4. **All the king's horses and all the king's men couldn't** <u>put Humpty Dumpty together again.</u>

    _____

5. **Some people believe paying taxes** <u>is actually a privilege.</u>

    _____

FITNESS

Please be aware of your environment and be safe at all times. If you cannot do an exercise, just try your best.

Repeat these **exercises 4 ROUNDS**

2 - Side Bending: 10 times to each side. Note: try to touch your feet.

3 - Tree Pose: Stay as long as possible. Note: do the same with the other leg.

1 - Squats: 15 times. Note: imagine you are trying to sit on a chair.

Word Problems: add/subtract/ multiply/divide

1. Alex had 1,634 toy cars in his collection. He sold three hundred and forty-six to his friend. How many toy cars does he have now?

2. Rachel bought three piñatas. One large piñata cost $ 21.96, a medium piñata cost $ 14.69 and the third piñata cost $ 11.44. How much did Rachel spend on piñatas?

 A. $47.59
 B. $47.89
 C. $48.09
 D. $48.49

3. Greg's brother had $12,356. He bought a laptop for $1,648, a wallet for $154, a coat for $368, and shoes for $125. How much money does he have left?

 A. $10,236
 B. $10,061
 C. $9,996
 D. $9,646

4. There are 6,785 small boxes on each shelf in a store. There are 16 shelves in total. How many small boxes are there in the store?

 A. 108,560
 B. 118,530
 C. 120,240
 D. 122,630

5. A bookstore ordered 565 new textbooks. If each textbook had 180 pages in it, how many pages are there total in all the textbooks?

6. In June 13,625 people visited the Broadway fair. In July 12,138 people visited the Broadway fair. How many people visited the Broadway fair in total for June and July?

7. Mrs. Torres has 45 rows of tomato plants. If she can get 1,356 tomatoes from each row, how many tomatoes would she have in total?

 A. 43,290
 B. 49,360
 C. 56,180
 D. 61,020

8. There are 378 jars of sour cream in Store A. Store B has 14 times more jars of sour cream than Store A. How many jars of sour cream does Store B have?

 A. 4,792
 B. 5,292
 C. 5,432
 D. 5,662

9. There are 1,542 cars in the parking lot. Each of them has 4 wheels. How many wheels in total are in the parking lot?

 A. 5,998
 B. 8,028
 C. 6,168
 D. 6,258

39

10. An entertainment hall at the mall is visited all day long. During the first hour, 1,542 people came in and 964 people left. During the second hour, 1,117 people came in and 863 people left. During the third hour, 975 people came in and 1,237 people left. How many people were still in the entertainment hall after 3 hours?

11. A packer can pack 1,524 cartons of juice an hour. If he works for 64 hours, how many cartons of juice would he have packed?

12. There are 12 problems on a page. There are 186 pages in a textbook. How many problems are there in a textbook?

    A. 2,342
    B. 2,232
    C. 2,192
    D. 1,932

13. Julia sold 2,328 hamburgers in a period of 24 days. If she sold an equal number of hamburgers everyday for the 24 days, how many hamburgers did she sell each day?

14. A cafe needed 2,730 coffee stickers. If each box has 65 coffee stickers in it, how many boxes will the cafe need to order?

15. Victoria types 80 words per minute. If she has to type 48 pages, where each page contains 200 words, how much time will she need?

16. Jack has a photo album that can store 8 photos per page. The photo album has a total of 42 pages, however, 5 of the pages have been badly damaged so they were removed. What is the total number of photos Jack can fit in the photo album?

17. There were 1,548 gallons of milk in a factory. They sold 1,137 gallons. How many gallons of milk remain unsold in the factory?

 FITNESS

Today you get to decide what fitness activity you would like to do!

Diagrams: add/subtract/ multiply/divide

1. Use the model below to solve the problem 744 + 568.

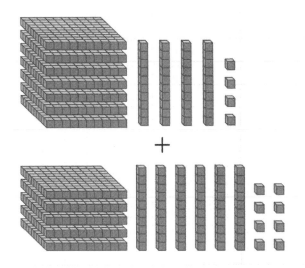

2. Use the model below to write an addition sentence.

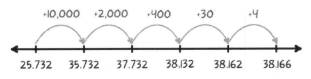

3. Which relationship could be shown by the model below?

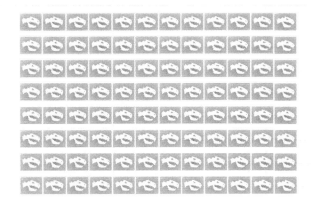

A. $2 \div 8 = 96$
B. $12 \times 8 = 96$
C. $12 + 8 = 96$
D. $96 \times 8 = 12$

4. Which equation is NOT shown by the model below?

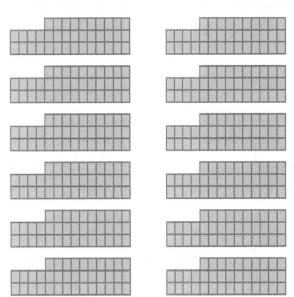

A. $38 \times 12 = 456$
B. $12 \times 38 = 456$
C. $38 + 12 = 456$
D. $456 \div 12 = 38$

5. Write a multiplication sentence to the model below.

6. Use the shapes to answer the question. How many groups of **9** can you make with the **54** shapes below?

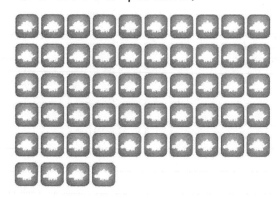

7. Use the model below to write a subtraction sentence.

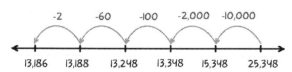

	-2	-60	-100	-2,000	-10,000
13,186	13,188	13,248	13,348	15,348	25,348

FITNESS

Please be aware of your environment and be safe at all times. If you cannot do an exercise, just try your best.

Repeat these **exercises 4 ROUNDS**

1 - High Plank: 20 sec.

2 - Chair: 15 sec.
Note: sit on an imaginary chair, keep your back straight.

3 - Waist Hooping: 15 times. Note: if you do not have a hoop, pretend you have an imaginary hoop and rotate your hips 10 times.

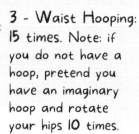

4 - Abs: 15 times

Place Value

1. In 673,194 which digit is in the ten thousands place?

A. 6 C. 3
B. 7 D. 1

2. In which of the following numbers is the digit 7 in the greatest place value?

A. 534,679
B. 236,891
C. 175,246
D. 134,765

3. Find and choose a pair of numbers in which the digit 5 differs by a factor of 1000.

A. 234,756 and 253,861
B. 623,549 and 153,764
C. 57,239 and 429,753
D. 437,285 and 256,341

4. In what place value is 8 in the number 5,769,843?

A. Tens
B. Hundreds
C. Thousands
D. Ten thousands

5. Which digit represents the thousands place in the number 673,198?

A. 3 C. 7
B. 6 D. 8

6. Denise wrote a number in which the digit 7 has the lowest value. Which number did she write?

A. 723,894
B. 891,756
C. 437,981
D. 249,673

7. What is the value of the underlined digit in 3,7̲84,126?

A. 7,000
B. 70,000
C. 700,000
D. 7,000,000

8. Determine the number shown in the boxes.

Milions	Hundred Thousands	Ten Thousands	Thousands	Hundreds	Tens	Ones
●●	●●●	●●●●●●●●	●	●●●●●	●●●●●●	●●●●●●●

_____

9. How many times greater is the number 600,000 than the number 600?

_____

10. The hundreds place value in the number 639,137 is:

_____

43

11. Determine the numbers shown in the boxes.

Ones	Tenths	Hundredths	Thousandths
•••	••• •••	••• ••	•••• •••

12. What is the value of the underlined digit in the number 2,6<u>5</u>8,913?

   A. 500,000
   B. 50,000
   C. 5,000
   D. 500

13. Write the missing number.
6 ten thousands + 7 thousands + _____ hundreds + 4 tens + 3 ones = 67,243.

   A. 1
   B. 2
   C. 3
   D. 4

14. What is the millions place digit in the number 8,937,654?

15. Which digit represents the thousandths place in the number 6.357?

   A. 3   C. 6
   B. 5   D. 7

16. In the number 7.398, the digit 7 is in what place value?

   A. Ones
   B. Tenths
   C. Hundredths
   D. Thousandths

17. Write a number with: 6 hundreds, 5 tens, 8 ten thousands, 7 ones, 3 millions, 6 hundred thousands.

   A. 6,830,567
   B. 3,680,657
   C. 3,608,657
   D. 3,760,856

YOGA

Please be aware of your environment and be safe at all times. If you cannot do an exercise, just try your best.

1 - Down Dog: 25 sec.

2 - Bend Down: 25 sec.

3 - Chair: 20 sec.

4 - Child Pose: 25 sec.

5 - Shavasana: as long as you can. Note: think of happy moments and relax your mind.

EXPERIMENT

Comparing the Density of Liquids

Last week, we used water to explore the concept of **density**. We saw that solid objects would sink or float based on whether they were more or less **dense** than water. This week, compare a number of different liquids and see how they react when placed near liquids of different densities.

Materials:

* I jar with a lid
* I bottle of dish soap
* I bottle of cooking oil
* I bottle of light corn syrup
* Room temperature water
* A few drops of food coloring (optional)
* A measuring cup
* A small funnel (optional)

Procedure:

1. Make sure your jar is clean and completely dry.

2. Using the measuring cup and/or funnel to avoid spillage, pour about an inch of the corn syrup into the bottom of the jar. If you want, you can gently stir in some food coloring to make things look more exciting! (**Note**: If you're using a funnel, be sure to clean and dry it after each time you pour one of the liquids through it.)

3. Next, pour a layer of dish soap into the jar, using your measuring cups and funnel as necessary. You can gently tilt the jar from side to side to ensure your layers are even, but be sure **not** to shake the jar.

4. Add a few drops of food coloring to your water, then add it to the jar to create a new layer. Again, be sure not to shake the jar – you don't want to create a bunch of soap bubbles in there.

5. Using your measuring cup or funnel, add a level of cooking oil to the top of the jar. If you want, you can add some food coloring to it ahead of time, but make sure to use a different color than what you used for the water.

6. Seal the jar tightly using its lid.

7. Observe how the different colored layers remain distinct as you turn the jar and view it from different angles. You can rotate the jar to watch the layers move, but make sure not to shake the jar until you're done with your observation. (You can do it afterwards, if you want, to see what happens!)

8. Be sure to talk to an adult about disposing of your jar safely afterwards. You don't want to just pour liquids like oil down the sink.

Follow-Up Questions:

1. Based on what you saw, what's one more liquid you know about that you predict would have a **high** density?

_____

_____

_____

2. Based on what you've seen, how is the concept of **density** connected to the fact that oil and water don't mix?

_____

_____

_____

 YOGA

Please be aware of your environment and be safe at all times. If you cannot do an exercise, just try your best.

2 - Down Dog: 25 sec.

3 - Stretching: Stay as long as possible.
Note: do on one leg then on another.

4 - Lower Plank: 12 sec.
Note: Keep your back straight and body tight.

1 - Tree Pose:
Stay as long as possible.
Note: do on one leg then on another.

6 - Shavasana: 5 min.
Note: this pose is very important and provides you with long term benefits. Try not to skip this. Close your eyes and imagine who you want to be and what your goals are! Always think happy thoughts.

5 - Book Pose: 15 sec.
Note: Keep your core tight. Legs should be across from your eyes.

Task: Yikes! There is a huge tangled mess. Match the correct letter with a number.

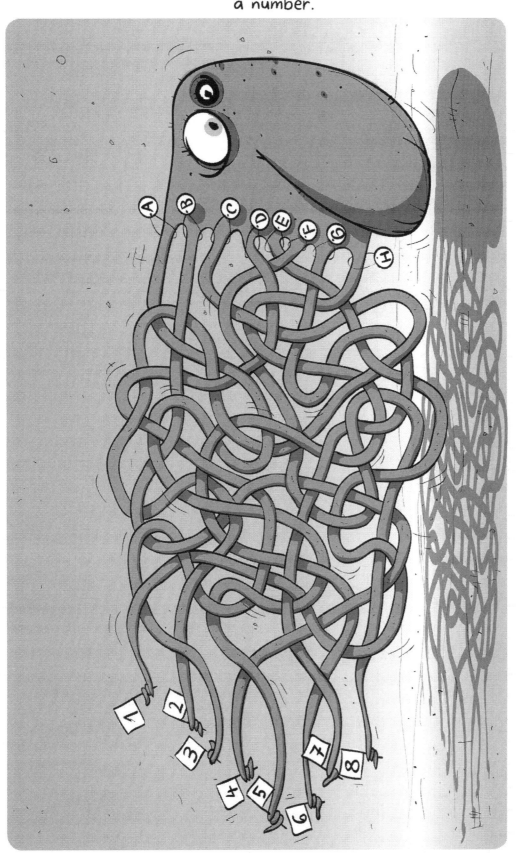

Oh yeah! Looks like you are getting the hang of this. Excited for Week 3? I know I sure am.

WEEK 3

Dinosaurs, although now extinct, have roamed the Earth for over 150 million years. It's widely believed by scientists that an asteroid hit the Yucatán Peninsula in Mexico which was a major cause of the extinction of dinosaurs.

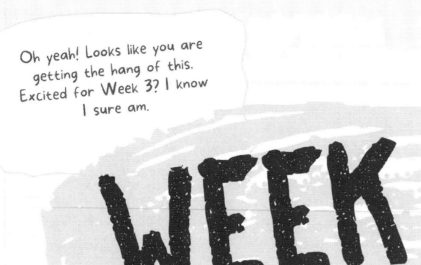

Simple Subject, Simple Predicate

Last week, we began breaking sentences into **subjects** and **predicates** in order to study and understand them more effectively. We began by dividing things into **complete subjects** and complete predicates. Remember, the **subject** contains all the information about who or what the sentence is about. The predicate contains information about what happens or what ideas about that subject are being communicated.

This week, we'll zero in on the **simple subject** and the simple predicate. Being able to find these words in a sentence gives you an instant sense of what's going on.

Key Terms

Complete Subject: The part of the sentence that identifies the person, place, thing, or idea that the sentence is about.

Complete Predicate: The part of the sentence that contains information about what action happened or what is going on. (What did the subject do? What is the subject like?)

Simple Subject: The noun (or nouns, if there is more than one subject) that best encapsulates exactly what person, place, thing, or idea the sentence is about.

Simple Predicate: The verb (action or linking) that encapsulates exactly what main action is going on.

Hint:

It's helpful to identify the **complete subject** and complete predicate first. Then, you can dive into picking which word from each provides the best sense of what's going on.

For Example...

In these sentences, the **complete subject** is in **bold** and the complete predicate is underlined. The **simple subject and predicate** are both *italicized*.

- ❋ **My rude, obnoxious *cousin*** *ruined* my birthday party.
  - * *Cousin* is the **simple subject** because, if you had to boil the whole subject down to one idea, it's describing the cousin.
  - * Ruined is the simple predicate because it describes what action the subject (cousin) performed.
- ❋ **The old railroad *bridge*** *collapsed* during the hurricane.
  - * *Bridge* is the **simple subject** because it's the one noun from the subject that best describes exactly what collapsed.
  - * Collapsed is the simple predicate because it is the main action occurring in the sentence.

From "The History of France"

By Charlotte M. Yonge

The country we now know as France is the tract of land shut in by the British Channel, the Bay of Biscay, the Pyrenees, the Mediterranean, and the Alps. But this country only gained the name of France by degrees.

In the earliest days of which we have any account, it was peopled by the Celts, and it was known to the Romans as part of a larger country which bore the name of Gaul. After all of it, save the north-western moorlands, or what we now call Brittany, had been conquered and settled by the Romans, it was overrun by tribes of the great Teutonic race, the same family to which Englishmen belong. Of these tribes, the Goths settled in the provinces to the south; the Burgundians, in the east, around the Jura; while the Franks, coming over the rivers in its unprotected north-eastern corner, and making themselves masters of a far wider territory, broke up into two kingdoms—that of the Eastern Franks in what is now Germany, and that of the Western Franks reaching from the Rhine to the Atlantic.

These Franks subdued all the other Teutonic conquerors of Gaul, while they adopted the religion, the language, and some of the civilization of the Romanized Gauls who became their subjects. Under the second Frankish dynasty, the Empire was renewed in the West, where it had been for a time put an end to by these Teutonic invasions, and the then Frankish king, Charles the Great, took his place as Emperor at its head. But in the time of his grandsons the various kingdoms and nations of which the Empire was composed, fell apart again under different descendants of his.

One of these, Charles the Bald, was made King of the Western Franks in what was termed the Neustrian, or "not eastern," kingdom, from which the present France has sprung. This kingdom in name covered all the country west of the Upper Meuse, but practically the Neustrian king had little power south of the Loire; and the Celts of Brittany were never included in it.

Tyrannosaurus

Our home, Earth, is the third planet from the sun and the only world known to support an atmosphere with free oxygen, oceans of liquid water on the surface and - the big one - life!

1. Based on the passage, who are some of the ancient groups that called France home?

_____

_____

2. Why was Rome important to the development of France?

_____

_____

3. Based on the passage, which of these things happened first?

   A. Charles the Bald became king of the Western Franks
   B. The Romans called the area "Gaul"
   C. The Celts settled in what is now known as France
   D. The Franks divided their territory into two kingdoms

4. What is the purpose of Paragraph 1 in the text?

   A. To generally introduce the topic of France
   B. To explain the origins of the French people
   C. To get the reader interested in the topic of French history
   D. The give the reader a sense of how France is defined geographically

5. How does the rest of the passage back up the author's opening claim that what we know as "France" only became France "by degrees" (meaning a little at a time)?

_____

_____

_____

_____

_____

Identifying Complete & Simple Subjects and Predicates

Directions: First, read each sentence below and draw a line with your pen or pencil between the **complete subject** and <u>complete predicate</u> of each sentence. Then, **circle** the **simple subject** and the <u>simple predicate</u>.

1. All cows eat grass.

2. George Washington and his troops camped in Valley Forge for about six months in 1777 and 1778.

3. My sister Malory learned to type using online software.

4. The biggest and most impressive carnival we went to last summer was at the state fair.

5. The long caravan of weekend cyclists caused major problems for everybody driving down the scenic highway.

FITNESS

Please be aware of your environment and be safe at all times. If you cannot do an exercise, just try your best.

Repeat these **exercises 4 ROUNDS**

2 - Lunges: 4 times to each leg.
Note: Use your body weight or books as weight to do leg lunges.

4 - Run: 50m
Note: Run 25 meters to one side and 25 meters back to the starting position.

1 - Abs: 15 times

From "The History of France"

By Charlotte M. Yonge

(Continued from Day One's Passage)

The great danger which this Neustrian kingdom had to meet came from the Northmen, or as they were called in England the Danes. These ravaged in Neustria as they ravaged in England; and a large part of the northern coast, including the mouth of the Seine, was given by Charles the Bald to Rolf or Rollo, one of their leaders, whose land became known as the Northman's land, or Normandy.

What most checked the ravages of these pirates was the resistance of Paris, a town which commanded the road along the river Seine; and it was in defending the city of Paris from the Northmen, that a warrior named Robert the Strong gained the trust and affection of the inhabitants of the Neustrian kingdom. He and his family became Counts (i.e., judges and protectors) of Paris, and Dukes (or leaders) of the Franks. Three generations of them were really great men—Robert the Strong, Odo, and Hugh the White; and when the descendants of Charles the Great had died out, a Duke of the Franks, Hugh Capet, was in 987 crowned King of the Franks.

All the after kings of France down to Louis Philippe were descendants of Hugh Capet. By this change, however, he gained little in real power; for, though he claimed to rule over the whole country of the Neustrian Franks, his authority was little heeded, save in the domain which he had possessed as Count of Paris, including the cities of Paris, Orleans, Amiens, and Rheims (the coronation place). He was guardian, too, of the great Abbeys of St. Denys and St. Martin of Tours. The Duke of Normandy and the Count of Anjou to the west, the Count of Flanders to the north, the Count of Champagne to the east, and the Duke of Aquitaine to the south, paid him homage, but were the only actual rulers in their own domains.

Tyrannosaurus REX

The T-Rex was an incredible meat-eating dinosaur that had a life span of about 30 years. The T-Rex once used to roam North America!

53

1. How was the city of **Paris** important to this point in French history?

   _____

   _____

2. Who were the Northmen, and why were they important to French history?

   _____

   _____

3. Based on the passage, which of these groups acted like pirates?

   A. The Neustrians
   B. The Danes
   C. The Franks
   D. The Parisians

4. Which of these best divides the first sentence of Paragraph 3 into its subject and predicate?

   A. All the after kings of France / down to Louis Philippe were descendants of Hugh Capet.
   B. All the after kings / of France down to Louis Philippe were descendants of Hugh Capet.
   C. All the after kings of France down to Louis Philippe /were descendants of Hugh Capet.
   D. All the after kings of France down to Louis Philippe were descendants / of Hugh Capet.

5. Based on the text, why did Hugh Capet not have much power, even though he was king?

   _____

   _____

   _____

   _____

   _____

Identifying Subjects and Predicates Part 2

Directions: First, read each sentence below and draw a line with your pen or pencil between the **complete subject** and <u>complete predicate</u> of each sentence. Then, **circle** the **simple subject** and the <u>simple predicate.</u>

1. Tonya's beautiful wedding gown sparkled in the sunlight as she walked down the aisle.

2. Mikael, our foreign exchange student, has an impressive collection of rocks and geodes from around the world.

3. The idea that all rivers flow south is a major misconception among students.

4. Hands-on projects provide young learners with opportunities to demonstrate what they know and what they're capable of.

5. The family of inexperienced campers accidentally started a small forest fire when they didn't dispose of ashes properly.

FITNESS

Please be aware of your environment and be safe at all times. If you cannot do an exercise, just try your best.

Repeat these **exercises** **4 ROUNDS**

2 - Side Bending: 10 times to each side. Note: try to touch your feet.

3 - Tree Pose: Stay as long as possible. Note: do the same with the other leg.

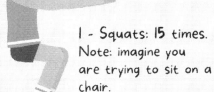

1 - Squats: 15 times. Note: imagine you are trying to sit on a chair.

TYRANNOSAURUS REX

Evaluating Expressions

1. What is $23 \times (42 + 17)$?

   A. 1,268
   B. 1,192
   C. 1,266
   D. 1,357

2. Solve the problem $(228 + 149) \times 9$.

   A. 2,963
   B. 3,393
   C. 3,423
   D. 3,783

3. Find $(6,265 - 3,722) \times 16$.

   A. 36,976
   B. 38,188
   C. 40,688
   D. 42,566

4. Calculate $(234 - 45) \times (122 - 86)$.

   _____

5. What is $(584 + 256) \div 24$?

   _____

6. Solve: $(922 - 47) \div 7$

   _____

7. Solve the problems below.

   A. $92 \times (135 + 216)$ _____
   B. $490 \div (86 - 51)$ _____
   C. $32 \times (12 + 68) \div 2$ _____
   D. $(27 + 31) \times (45 + 14)$ _____

8. What is $(324 + 826) \div (98 - 73)$?

   A. 32
   B. 46
   C. 54
   D. 62

9. What is the missing number $(453 + \underline{\hspace{2cm}}) \div 16 = 43$?

   A. 186
   B. 198
   C. 235
   D. 248

10. Which equation is FALSE?

    A. $(654 - 127) \times 45 = 23,715$
    B. $975 \div (346 - 321) = 39$
    C. $22 \times (1,965 - 278) = 37,114$
    D. $(5,297 - 1,265) \div 36 = 114$

11. Find $(6,732 - 1,257) \times (129 - 36)$.

    _____

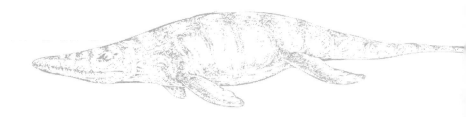

12. Which equation is true?

    A. $(1,299 + 3,563) \div 22 = 221$
    B. $16 \times (132 + 34) \times 12 = 32,872$
    C. $(65 + 78) \times (45 - 29) = 2,188$
    D. $(1,444 - 349) \div (457 - 238) = 6$

13. What are the missing numbers in the following equations?

$25 \times (157 + \underline{\hspace{3cm}}) = 8,850$

$\underline{\hspace{3cm}} \div (453 - 425) = 135$

14. Solve $(56 + 69) \times (268 - 137)$.

15. Find $9,144 \div (2,784 - 2,748)$.

16. Calculate $(72 + 126) \div (687 - 654)$.

17. What is $22 \times (562 + 733)$?

18. What is the missing number $48 \times (\underline{\hspace{2cm}} - 239) = 4,272$?

19. Solve: $(794 + 718) \div (68 - 41)$

20. What is $(58 \times 89) + (192 \div 16)$?

FITNESS

Please be aware of your environment and be safe at all times. If you cannot do an exercise, just try your best.

Repeat these **exercises 4 ROUNDS**

2 - Lunges: 7 times to each leg.
Note: Use your body weight or books as weight to do leg lunges.

4 - Abs: 15 times

1 - Bend forward: 15 times.
Note: try to touch your feet. Make sure to keep your back straight and if needed you can bend your knees.

3 - Plank: 20 sec.

Patterns

1. Which rule describes the pattern 3, 12, 21, 30, ...?

    A. Add 8
    B. Add 9
    C. Times 3
    D. Times 4

2. Which rule describes the pattern 8, 32, 128, 512, ...?

    A. Add 22
    B. Add 24
    C. Times 3
    D. Times 4

3. What is the next number in this pattern 1, 4, 10, 19, 31, ...?

    A. 44
    B. 45
    C. 46
    D. 47

4. Fill in the next number in this pattern: 3, 15, 75, 375, ...

5. What is the next number in this pattern 75, 60, 47, 36, 27, ...?

    A. 20
    B. 21
    C. 22
    D. 23

6. What is the missing number in this pattern 12, 48, 192, ..., 3,072?

7. Which expression shows the relationship between the input and the output?

Input (x)	12	20	45	53	68
Output (y)	16	24	49	57	72

    A. $x + 8 = y$
    B. $x + 4 = y$
    C. $x + 16 = y$
    D. $x = y + 4$

8. Write an equation to show the relationship between the input and the output.

Input (x)	26	35	41	58	66
Output (y)	14	23	29	46	54

9. Which expression shows the relationship between **k** and **m**?

k	m
12	1
36	3
48	4
72	6

    A. $k - 11 = m$
    B. $k \times 3 = m$
    C. $k \times 12 = m$
    D. $k \div 12 = m$

10. Write an equation which shows the relationship between **k** and **m**.

k	m
4	16
13	52
52	208
71	284

Answer _____

11. Fill in the missing cells in the table below.

Input (x)	2		7	9		22
Output (y)	13	17	18	20	26	

12. Fill in the missing cells in the table below.

Input (x)	12	39		72	99	
Output (y)	4	13	16		33	43

13. Fill in the patterns and then graph the coordinate pairs, using the rule "x: start at 2 and add 2. y: start at 3 and add 1".

x				
y				

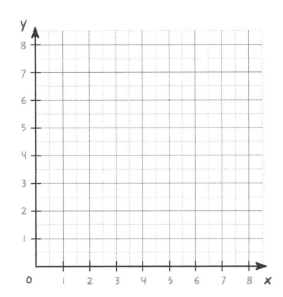

FITNESS

Please be aware of your environment and be safe at all times. If you cannot do an exercise, just try your best.

Repeat these **exercises 4 ROUNDS**

1 - High Plank: 20 sec.

2 - Chair: 15 sec. Note: sit on an imaginary chair, keep your back straight.

3 - Waist Hooping: 15 times. Note: if you do not have a hoop, pretend you have an imaginary hoop and rotate your hips 10 times.

4 - Abs: 15 times

Comparing numbers and decimals

1. Compare 8,976,235 and 8,976,251, using a comparison symbol.

_____

2. Which statement is true?

A. 234,892 > 234,896
B. 7,561,902 < 7,560,989
C. 8,983 = 8.983
D. 5.4363 < 5,436.3

3. Which number is greater than 6.324?

A. 6.288
B. 1.7329
C. 7.01
D. 3.8976

4. Put comparison symbols for each pair of decimals.

A. 5.672 and 5.677 _____
B. 46.872 and 4.978 _____
C. 0.187 and 0.065 _____
D. 56.709 and 476.98 _____

5. Which statement is FALSE?

A. 435,987 < 435,991
B. 65.091 > 65.108
C. 0.096 > 0.0918
D. 6.952 < 69.52

6. Which number is smaller than 8,986.752?

A. 8,986.763
B. 8,986.659
C. 8,987.542
D. 8,986.773

7. Evaluate the following number sentences and use a comparison symbol to compare the two numbers..

A. 8,706 + 2,308 and 6,968 + 3,962

_____

B. 235 × 12 and 314 × 16

_____

C. 46 × 27 and 78 × 11

_____

D. 3,486 − 1,592 and 6,943 − 4,116

_____

8. Which number sentence is true?

A. 0.354 > 0.362
B. 7,983 < 7,991
C. 87.935 > 765.34
D. 65,973.983 > 660,738.56

9. Compare 56.932 and 56.8765, using a comparison symbol.

_____

10. Order the numbers from smallest to greatest: 6.954, 6.732, 65.43, 59.347.

_____

11. Compare the following pairs of numbers and decimals.

A. 56 and 56.128 _____
B. 472 and 47.289 _____
C. 8,934.278 and 8,934,209 _____
D. 7.008 and 7.100 _____

12. Order the decimals from greatest to smallest. 3.781, 24.956, 3.803. 134.27, 46.01.

_____

13. Which number is greater than 0.357?

   A. 0.298
   B. 0.342
   C. 0.089
   D. 0.408

14. Evaluate the following number sentences and use a comparison symbol to compare the two numbers.

   A. 25×64 and 68×23

   _____

   B. $248 + 127$ and $563 - 329$

   _____

   C. $556 + 348$ and $499 + 455$

   _____

   D. 86×16 and 92×11

15. Compare the product of 46×17 and 812, using a comparison symbol.

   _____

16. Which number is greater than the quotient of 1,683 and 9?

   A. 178   C. 190
   B. 184   D. 168

17. Compare the following pairs of decimals, using a comparison symbol.

   A. 4.932 and 5.068 _____
   B. 34.76 and 3.489 _____
   C. 12.956 and 1,134.9 _____
   D. 6.096 and 6.132 _____

18. Which number is equal to the difference of 1,835 and 973?

   A. 892   C. 872
   B. 862   D. 882

YOGA

Please be aware of your environment and be safe at all times. If you cannot do an exercise, just try your best.

1 - Down Dog: 25 sec.

2 - Bend Down: 25 sec.

3 - Chair: 20 sec.

4 - Child Pose: 25 sec.

5 - Shavasana: as long as you can. Note: think of happy moments and relax your mind.

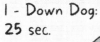

Observing Your Heart's Activity

Your heart is one of the most important organs in your entire body, but if you're a young, healthy person, you probably aren't even aware of its function unless you do a lot of running. Your heart works as a **pump** that pushes blood out from your core to the various parts of your body. That blood carries oxygen that your body needs to function. Today, we'll look at some simple ways you can explore your heart in action.

Materials:

* * I timer or stopwatch
* * Notepaper
* * A comfortable place to sit
* * A small indoor or outdoor area that is clear and safe for physical activity

Procedure:

1. Make three columns on your notepaper. Label the top of one **Chest**, the top of the next one **Wrist**, and the top of the third one as **Neck.**

2. Find a comfortable place to sit and take a few minutes to focus on relaxing and clearing your head.

3. Once you're feeling relaxed, take your right hand and place it over the left side of your chest until you can feel your heartbeat. There should be a light "lub-dub" feeling. If you're having trouble finding your heartbeat at first, closing your eyes and pressing down lightly with your hand can help.

4. After you've found your heartbeat, set your timer for **one minute** and count how many times you feel your heart beat in that sixty seconds. When the timer goes off, write down how many beats you felt in the **Chest** column.

5. Take a few seconds to relax again, and allow yourself to sit with your arms hanging downward (this will make the next step easier).

6. Place your hands in your lap with your palms up. Using the index and middle fingers of your right hand, reach across and press down on the **outside** of your left wrist. Feel around the underside of your wrist directly below the base of your thumb until you find your heartbeat again. This is technically called your radial pulse. (Again, if you're having trouble finding this spot, closing your eyes and pressing firmly will help. This will be a little tougher than just putting your hand over your chest.)

7. Once you've found the spot, set your timer for **one minute** again and count how many beats you feel in your wrist during that time. When the timer goes off, mark the number of beats in the **Wrist** column.

8. Take another second to relax. Then, when you feel ready, using the same two fingers you used to find your **radial pulse**, reach up under the corner of your jaw (on the same side as the hand you're using), and lightly press in against the side of your neck. You should be able to feel your heartbeat one more time. This is called your **carotid pulse**. Again, closing your eyes and pressing in firmly will make this easier to find.

9. Once you're comfortable locating your carotid pulse, set your timer for **one minute** and count how many beats you feel in your neck during that time. When the timer goes off, mark the number of beats in the **Neck** column.

10. Go to a place that's safe for vigorous activity and play for 10 minutes. You can do whatever indoor or outdoor fitness activity feels right for you: jumping jacks, skipping rope, playing soccer, or just running around are all great activities. The goal is to do something really vigorous, though – so whatever you do, make sure you go all out.

11. After you've exercised for 10 minutes, return to the area where your notepaper and time are located and **measure your heartbeat/pulse at all three locations again**: your chest, your neck, and your wrist. Count beats at each spot for **one minute**, just like before. As you do each one, you'll probably notice your heart rate going down as your body recovers from your workout. Document each number of beats on your paper.

12. Give yourself another 15 minutes to cool down fully (having a drink of water is a great idea!), then check your pulse for a third and final time at all three locations: chest, wrist, and neck. Mark down your final readings in all three columns, then compare the three sets of numbers. Think about how your first and third numbers compare and how they are both different from the ones immediately after your workout.

Follow-Up Questions:

1. Which of the three spots did you find it most difficult to feel your pulse? What strategies did you use to make sure you were able to measure it?

_____

_____

2. Based on what you observed, what do you predict is the **relationship** between your **heartbeat** and **physical activity**?

_____

_____

Please be aware of your environment and be safe at all times. If you cannot do an exercise, just try your best.

YOGA

1 - Tree Pose: Stay as long as possible. Note: do on one leg then on another.

2 - Down Dog: 25 sec.

4 - Lower Plank: 12 sec. Note: Keep your back straight and body tight.

3 - Stretching: Stay as long as possible. Note: do on one leg then on another.

5 - Book Pose: 15 sec. Note: Keep your core tight. Legs should be across from your eyes.

Task: Match the corresponding letter to the number for the maze below.

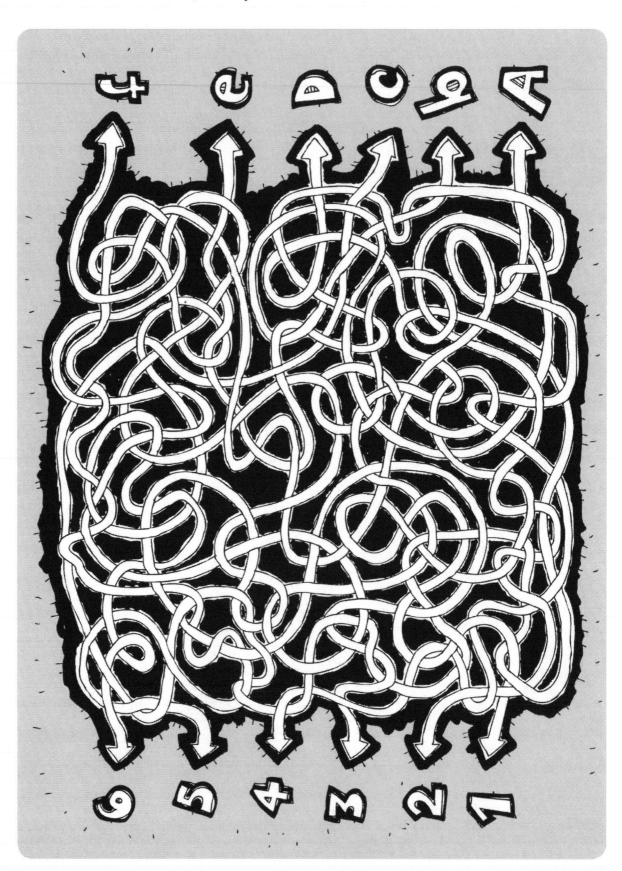

Rock on!
Practicing math and English concepts is just as important as keeping our body healthy and active. Have you tried our fitness activities?

WEEK 4

Thanks to palaeontologists, scientists who study fossils and dinosaurs, our knowledge of dinosaurs continues to grow. There are hundreds and hundreds of dinosaur species and more is yet to be discovered!

Conjunctions

We've started exploring sentence structure by breaking short, fairly simple sentences down and identifying their parts. However, if we're going to start writing and understanding longer, more complex sentences, we need to get acquainted with the words we use to connect ideas. We call those words **conjunctions!**

This week, we'll look at three different types of conjunctions: coordinating, subordinating, and correlative!

Key Terms

Coordinating Conjunctions: The three most basic connecting words – and, but, or
Subordinating Conjunctions: Connecting words that attempt to show the relationships between ideas. For example...

Because	While	Since	Though	If
Although	When	As	Even if	Even though

Correlative Conjunctions: Pairs of conjunctions that always work as partners

- ✼ **Either… or:** Used to show a choice between two things
- ✼ **Neither… nor:** Used to show that none of the options are satisfactory
- ✼ **Not only… but also:** Used to add additional information for emphasis
- ✼ **Both… and:** Used to show two things are equally true or valid

For Example...

- ✼ Freddy seems like an intimidating guy, **but** he is actually very nice.
  - * **But** is a conjunction, specifically a **coordinating conjunction** that's connecting these two ideas (that Freddy seems intimidating **but** is nice).

- ✼ Raphael **and** James participated in the chicken wing eating contest.
  - * **And** is a **coordinating conjunction** that's showing that two people both did the contest.

- ✼ You need to **either** empty the dishwasher **or** straighten up the living room.
  - * **Either...or** is used as a set of **correlative conjunctions** to show that there is a choice between two options.

- ✼ All the fifth graders had to stay inside **because** several students had been rude to the lunch lady.
  - * **Because** is used as a **subordinating conjunction** that shows the connection between these two sentences. It shows one idea (staying inside) is the direct result of the other (being rude to the lunch ladies).

From "Studies of Trees"

By Jacob Joshua Levison

The Larch & The Cypress

How to tell them from other trees: In summer the larch and cypress may easily be told from other trees by their leaves. These are needle-shaped and arranged in clusters with numerous leaves to each cluster in the case of the larch, and feathery and flat in the case of the cypress. In winter, when their leaves have dropped off, the trees can be told by their cones, which adhere to the branches.

There are nine recognized species of larch and two of bald cypress. The larch is characteristically a northern tree, growing in the northern and mountainous regions of the northern hemisphere from the Arctic circle to Pennsylvania in the New World, and in Central Europe, Asia, and Japan in the Old World. It forms large forests in the Alps of Switzerland and France.

The European larch and not the American is the principal species considered here, because it is being planted extensively in this country and in most respects is preferable to the American species.

The bald cypress is a southern tree of ancient origin, the well-known cypress of Montezuma in the gardens of Chepultepec having been a species of Taxodium. The tree is now confined to the swamps and river banks of the South Atlantic and Gulf States, where it often forms extensive forests to the exclusion of all other trees. In those regions along the river swamps, the trees are often submerged for several months of the year.

How to tell them from each other: In summer the larch may be told from the cypress by its leaves. In winter the two can be distinguished by their characteristic forms. The larch is a broader tree as compared with the cypress and its form is more conical. The cypress is more slender and it is taller. The two have been grouped together in this study because they are both coniferous trees and, unlike the other Conifers, are both deciduous, their leaves falling in October.

1. Based on this format, **what other information** do you expect might be contained in the book this passage is from?

_____

_____

2. How can you tell the difference between a larch and a cypress in the **winter**?

_____

_____

3. Which of these best describes the **overall purpose** of this passage?

   A. To help people figure out how to identify Larch and Cypress trees
   B. To convince people the European larch is better than the American larch
   C. To show people how the habitats of these plants are under threat
   D. To describe the different species of larch and cypress

4. What is the role of Paragraph **2** within the overall passage?

   A. To help the reader understand what these trees look like
   B. To help the reader understand where these trees are located
   C. To help the reader understand how many species of cypress there are
   D. To help the reader understand the differences between cypresses and larches

5. Why do you think the author decided to introduce the cypress and the larch **in the same section?** What details from the text back up your answer?

_____

_____

_____

_____

APATOSAURUS

Identifying and Classifying Conjunctions

Directions: Read each sentence below and circle the conjunctions in each sentence. On the line below, identify whether the conjunctions you found were **coordinating, subordinating, or correlative.**

1. Someone almost got hit at the bus stop in all the fog and rain this morning.

_____

2. I must have left my keys at school because neither my father nor my mother has seen them.

_____

3. Nobody's sure who's been writing the graffiti on the boys' bathroom wall, even though it's been going on for months.

_____

4. Mr. Krebett doesn't give homework since he discovered that nobody was doing it.

_____

5. The teacher assumed most of the students had completed their assignment, as a large amount of off-topic chatter was going on around the room.

_____

FITNESS

Please be aware of your environment and be safe at all times. If you cannot do an exercise, just try your best.

Repeat these **exercises 4 ROUNDS**

2 - Lunges: 4 times to each leg.
Note: Use your body weight or books as weight to do leg lunges.

4 - Run: 50m
Note: Run 25 meters to one side and 25 meters back to the starting position.

1 - Abs: 15 times

3 - Plank: 20 sec.

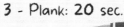

From "Studies of Trees"

By Jacob Joshua Levison

The Oaks & Chestnut

How to tell them from other trees: The oaks are rather difficult to identify and, in studying them it will often be necessary to look for more than one distinguishing character. The oaks differ from other trees in bearing acorns. Their leaves have many lobes and their upper lateral buds cluster at the top of the twigs. The general contour of each oak presents a characteristic branching and sturdiness uncommon in other trees.

The chestnut differs from other trees in bearing burs and its bark is also distinctly characteristic.

How to tell them from each other: There are two groups of oaks, the white oak and the black oak. The white oaks mature their acorns in one year and, therefore, only acorns of the same year can be found on trees of this group. The black oaks take two years in which to mature their acorns and, therefore, young acorns of the present year and mature acorns of the previous year may be found on the same tree at one time. The leaves of the white oaks have rounded margins and rounded lobes, while those of the black oaks have pointed margins and sharp pointed. The bark of the white oaks is light colored and breaks up in loose flakes, while that of the black oaks is darker and deeply ridged or tight. The white oak is the type of the white oak group and the black, red and pin oaks are types of the other. For the characterization of the individual species, the reader is referred to the following pages.

WHITE OAK (Quercus alba)

Distinguishing characters: The massive ramification of its branches is characteristic of this species and often an easy clue to its identification. The bark has a light gray color—lighter than that of the other oaks—and breaks into soft, loose flakes. The leaves are deeply lobed. The buds are small, round and congested at the end of the year's growth. The acorns usually have no stalks and are set in shallow, rough cups. The kernels of the acorns are white and palatable.

Form and size: The white oak grows into a large tree with a wide-spreading, massive crown, dissolving into long, heavy, twisted branches. When grown in the open it possesses a short sturdy trunk; in the forest its trunk is tall and stout.

Range: Eastern North America.

1. How can studying **acorns** be useful in telling a White Oak from a Black Oak?

_____

_____

2. Which details from the "Distinguishing Characters" sections help you understand what a White Oak **looks like?**

_____

_____

3. Based on the passage, where would you be **least** likely to see a White Oak?

   A. Massachusetts
   B. New York
   C. Pennsylvania
   D. Los Angeles

4. Which word in this sentence from Paragraph 4 is a **conjunction?** "_The massive ramification of its branches is characteristic of this species and often an easy clue to its identification._"

   A. Massive
   B. Characteristic
   C. And
   D. Its

5. What kind of **additional information** do you think would be helpful for the author to add? What would make this description **even more effective** for you?

_____

_____

_____

_____

_____

Choosing the Right Conjunction

Directions: Each sentence below contains a blank where a conjunction is needed. Read the sentence carefully, then fill in the blank by selecting one of the choices from the parentheses that follow the sentence. Remember, the correct conjunction should help the reader understand the relationships between ideas.

1. Neither Ethan, Chet, _____ Roger could manage a goal against Springfield's great soccer team. (OR / NOR / AND / BUT)

2. I was late for class _____ I ran as fast as I could. (BECAUSE / BUT / EVEN THOUGH / WHEN)

3. _____ did Chrissy eat an entire pizza, she also drank a whole pitcher of soda. (ALTHOUGH / NOT ONLY / WHETHER / REALLY)

4. The teacher gave the students the class celebration she'd promised, _____ everybody got an A on their geography quiz. (EVEN THOUGH / WHILE / AND / AS)

5. I used to think that most people were difficult to deal with, _____ then I learned that, with the right approach, dealing with people is actually fun. (AND / WHILE / BUT / AS WELL AS)

FITNESS

Please be aware of your environment and be safe at all times. If you cannot do an exercise, just try your best.

Repeat these **exercises 4 ROUNDS**

2 - Side Bending: 10 times to each side. Note: try to touch your feet.

3 - Tree Pose: Stay as long as possible. Note: do the same with the other leg.

1 - Squats: 15 times. Note: imagine you are trying to sit on a chair.

Word problems: add/subtract for fractions

1. Dylan bought two boxes of candied nuts. Their total weight was $5\frac{3}{4}$ kilograms. If he bought a third box that weighed $4\frac{2}{4}$ kilograms, what is the combined weight of all boxes Dylan bought?

2. Fred cut off $6\frac{3}{4}$ feet of white ribbon and Georgia cut off $2\frac{5}{6}$ feet of purple ribbon. What was the total length of the ribbons that were cut off?

3. Eddie ran $\frac{3}{8}$ of a mile and Henry ran $\frac{4}{5}$ of a mile. Find the difference between the distance they ran.

4. Bella drank $1\frac{2}{5}$ glasses of milk and Ben drank $1\frac{5}{9}$ glasses of milk. How much more did Ben drink?

5. The oak trees were planted on $\frac{1}{4}$ of the park and maple trees grew on $\frac{2}{5}$ of the park. What part of the park do these trees occupy in total?

6. Tina sold $8\frac{1}{4}$ kilograms of apples and $7\frac{5}{12}$ kilograms of plums she had gathered in the morning. How many kilograms more of apples did she sell than plums?

7. Nicky swam $\frac{4}{20}$ of a mile and Peter swam $\frac{6}{25}$ of a mile. What is the difference between the distance they swam?

8. Robert types $5\frac{4}{9}$ pages per hour and his father types $2\frac{7}{8}$ pages more than him per hour. How many pages do they type altogether in one hour?

9. Last week Mike spent $6\frac{3}{8}$ hours on solving math problems and his sister Sandra spent $5\frac{2}{5}$ hours on solving the same problems. How much more time did Mike spend on solving the problems than Sandra last week?

10. Mary ate $\frac{6}{10}$ lbs of peanuts and Joshua ate $\frac{6}{8}$ lbs of peanuts. How many lbs of peanuts did they eat altogether?

11. Vicky used $1\frac{3}{5}$ cups of sugar for a cake and $1\frac{5}{12}$ cups of sugar for pancakes. How much more sugar was used for the cake than the pancakes?

12. Mr. Clark used $6\frac{1}{4}$ acres of land for planting wheat. Mr. Matthews used $2\frac{3}{5}$ more than that amount of land. Which equation could be used to find out how many acres Mr. Matthews used for planting wheat?

A. $6\frac{1}{4} + 2\frac{3}{5} = 8\frac{4}{5}$

B. $6\frac{1}{4} + 2\frac{3}{5} = 8\frac{3}{15}$

C. $6\frac{1}{4} + 2\frac{3}{5} = 8\frac{17}{20}$

D. $6\frac{1}{4} + 2\frac{3}{5} = 8\frac{19}{20}$

13. Francis had **36** toys. He gave $\frac{5}{6}$ of his toys to an orphanage. How many toys does he have left?

14. Christopher worked for $2\frac{2}{6}$ hours on Tuesday. On Thursday he worked $1\frac{3}{5}$ hours longer than on Tuesday. How many hours did Christopher work on Thursday?

15. The recipe for cookies calls for $1\frac{2}{8}$ cups of cocoa powder. Rachel has only $\frac{3}{4}$ cups of cocoa. How much more cocoa does Rachel need to buy in order to make cookies?

FITNESS

Please be aware of your environment and be safe at all times. If you cannot do an exercise, just try your best.

Repeat these **exercises 4 ROUNDS**

I - Bend forward: 15 times.
Note: try to touch your feet. Make sure to keep your back straight and if needed you can bend your knees.

2 - Lunges: 7 times to each leg.
Note: Use your body weight or books as weight to do leg lunges.

4 - Abs: 15 times

3 - Plank: 20 sec.

Comparing fractions

1. Which of the following number sentences is true ?

A. $\frac{3}{7} > \frac{12}{25}$

B. $\frac{4}{9} < \frac{5}{12}$

C. $\frac{32}{25} = \frac{6}{5}$

D. $\frac{9}{15} > \frac{13}{28}$

2. Which symbol would make this inequality true?

$$\frac{3}{7} \rule{1cm}{0.4pt} \frac{4}{9}$$

A. >

B. <

C. =

D. +

3. Choose the missing fraction to make this number sentence true.

$$\frac{28}{5} < \rule{1.5cm}{0.4pt}$$

A. $\frac{17}{4}$

C. $\frac{13}{2}$

B. $\frac{14}{3}$

D. $\frac{36}{8}$

4. Which number sentence below is true?

A. $\frac{6}{9} = \frac{24}{36}$

B. $\frac{3}{11} > \frac{7}{22}$

C. $\frac{9}{16} > \frac{4}{5}$

D. $\frac{6}{13} > \frac{5}{10}$

5. Find the fraction that makes the number sentence true.

$$\frac{3}{7} < \rule{1.5cm}{0.4pt}$$

A. $\frac{2}{6}$

B. $\frac{6}{10}$

C. $\frac{4}{12}$

D. $\frac{5}{14}$

6. Determine which fraction shown below is less than $\frac{7}{16}$.

A. $\frac{14}{30}$

B. $\frac{5}{9}$

C. $\frac{13}{18}$

D. $\frac{8}{32}$

7. Which fraction can be used to make the number sentence true?

$$\rule{1.5cm}{0.4pt} > \frac{8}{12}$$

A. $\frac{4}{16}$

B. $\frac{14}{28}$

C. $\frac{14}{18}$

D. $\frac{9}{20}$

8. Which number sentence below is FALSE?

A. $\dfrac{25}{4} > \dfrac{38}{8}$

B. $\dfrac{5}{12} = \dfrac{15}{36}$

C. $\dfrac{7}{21} > \dfrac{16}{64}$

D. $\dfrac{6}{18} > \dfrac{15}{25}$

9. Which symbol would make this inequality true?

$$\dfrac{45}{8} \rule{1cm}{0.4pt} \dfrac{26}{4}$$

A. $>$ C. $=$

B. $<$ D. $+$

10. What is the missing fraction in this inequality?

$$\dfrac{39}{7} >$$

A. $\dfrac{26}{5}$ C. $\dfrac{59}{10}$

B. $\dfrac{45}{8}$ D. $\dfrac{18}{3}$

11. Compare $\dfrac{4}{9}$ and $\dfrac{3}{8}$, using a comparison symbol.

_____

12. Write a true number sentence, using a comparison symbol and the fractions $\dfrac{16}{20}$ and $\dfrac{24}{36}$.

_____

13. What number would complete the equation $\dfrac{2}{7} = \dfrac{14}{?}$?

_____

14. Use '>', '<', or '=' between $\dfrac{6}{14}$ and $\dfrac{9}{20}$ to solve the problem.

_____

15. Compare $\dfrac{13}{39}$ and $\dfrac{25}{75}$.

_____

FITNESS

Please be aware of your environment and be safe at all times. If you cannot do an exercise, just try your best.

Repeat these **exercises 4 ROUNDS**

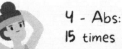

2 - Chair: 15 sec.
Note: sit on an imaginary chair, keep your back straight.

4 - Abs: 15 times

1 - High Plank: 20 sec.

3 - Waist Hooping: 15 times. Note: if you do not have a hoop, pretend you have an imaginary hoop and rotate your hips 10 times.

Shading in fraction models

1. Use the model to add $\frac{11}{24} + \frac{3}{8}$.

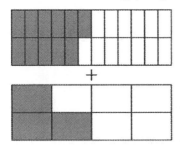

A. $\frac{6}{8}$ C. $\frac{20}{24}$

B. $\frac{19}{24}$ D. $\frac{7}{8}$

2. What is $\frac{6}{8} - \frac{2}{5}$?

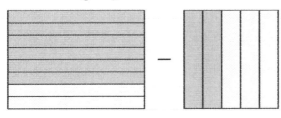

3. Use the model to add $\frac{3}{9} + \frac{7}{12}$.

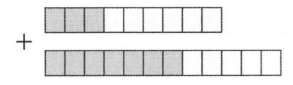

A. $\frac{6}{9}$ C. $\frac{9}{12}$

B. $\frac{9}{9}$ D. $\frac{11}{12}$

4. Solve the problem: $\frac{2}{3} + \frac{3}{6}$.

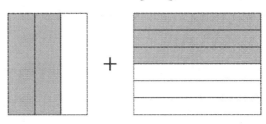

5. Use the model to solve $\frac{11}{15} - \frac{2}{5}$.

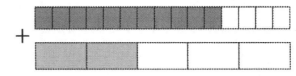

A. $\frac{3}{5}$ C. $\frac{4}{15}$

B. $\frac{5}{15}$ D. $\frac{2}{5}$

6. What is $3\frac{2}{8} + 4\frac{3}{6}$?

7. Solve the problem: $2\frac{3}{6} - 1\frac{11}{16}$, using the model below.

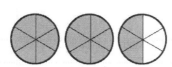

—

A. $\frac{5}{16}$ C. $\frac{13}{16}$

B. $1\frac{5}{16}$ D. $1\frac{4}{6}$

A. $4\frac{15}{18}$ C. $5\frac{15}{18}$

B. $4\frac{17}{18}$ D. $5\frac{11}{18}$

9. Solve the problem: $\frac{4}{6} + \frac{4}{10}$.

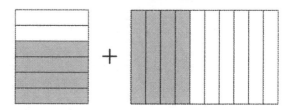

8. Use the model to add $2\frac{5}{6}$ to $2\frac{14}{18}$.

+

10. What is $\frac{7}{9} - \frac{3}{5}$?

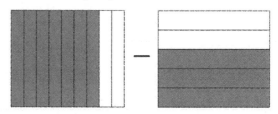

YOGA

Please be aware of your environment and be safe at all times. If you cannot do an exercise, just try your best.

1 - Down Dog: 25 sec.

2 - Bend Down: 25 sec.

3 - Chair: 20 sec.

4 - Child Pose: 25 sec.

5 - Shavasana: as long as you can. Note: think of happy moments and relax your mind.

WEEK 4 DAY 6 — EXPERIMENT

The Heart as a Pump

Last week, we used some exercise and observation to study how our heart works as a pump to move blood to different parts of the body. However, what we weren't able to do was see how the heart actually works to push that blood around effectively. This week, we'll create a model to help us understand what's going on inside our bodies. Our human heart has **four chambers**: two **atria** and two **ventricles**. Today, we'll make a scaled down heart with **one atrium and one ventricle**.

Materials:

* 3 empty, clean, dry 20oz plastic bottles
* At least 4 flexible/bending drinking straws
* Masking tape
* Cool, running water

* A large container (like a bowl or pitcher)
* A few drops of food coloring (preferably red)
* A drill (and **an adult** to use it!)
* Some sort of clay, putty, or dough (to form a tight seal)

Procedure:

1. Begin by **finding an adult** who is good with tools to help you get set up.

2. Take the caps off all three plastic bottles. Set one of them aside as a back-up. Then, **having an adult** use the drill, create two small holes the diameter of the drinking straws in each of the two remaining caps. The goal is to create as tight a seal as possible, so you want to create the smallest possible hole that the straw will fit through.

3. Insert a straw through the first hole in one of the caps and leave the other one empty. Push the straw through so that when you screw it onto the bottle, it will be hanging down into the liquid below.

4. Slide a second straw into the top of the one you just threaded through the cap so that the bendable parts of the straws are closest to where they join (you may need to pinch it a little to do this).

5. Insert the bottom end of the straw you just added through one of the holes in the second bottle cap.

6. Join two straws, like you did in Step 4, and insert the long end of one of them into the second hole of the second bottlecap. You should know have a setup with two bottlecaps: one with one straw going through it and connecting to the second bottlecap, which should have a second straw coming out the other hole.

7. Fill your bowl or pitcher with room temperature water and add the red food coloring to make it look like blood.

8. Fill <u>two</u> of your bottles at least three-quarters full with the blood mixture you've just made. Then, screw the two caps with the straws attached onto them. At this time, you can add some clay or putty around the places where the straws go into the caps to make sure your seals are tight.

9. Take your third bottle (the one that is still empty) and, leaving the cap off, insert the free end of the drinking straw that you created in Step 6 into it. This three-bottle setup is your model heart! The first bottle (with the one straw coming out of it) represents the **atrium**, where blood enters the heart. The second bottle (with two straws coming out of it) represents the **ventricle**, which actually pumps the blood out to your body. The third, empty bottle, represents the rest of your body, where the blood is going.

10. Squeeze the bridge of straws between the **atrium** bottle and the **ventricle** bottle. After a few seconds, you should see blood start to flow from the atrium and into the ventricle.

11. Then, squeeze the straw bridge between the **ventricle** bottle and the **body** bottle. You should see blood flow freely.

12. Squeeze the straws between the different chambers of your heart and see how much of the blood you can move between the bottles.

Follow-Up Questions:

1. Based on this experiment, why does the heart need both the **atrium** and the **ventricle** to be working well?

_____

_____

2. What does the importance of **seals** and **tight connections** in this experiment tell you about the way the heart works?

_____

YOGA

Please be aware of your environment and be safe at all times. If you cannot do an exercise, just try your best.

2 - Down Dog: 25 sec.

3 - Stretching: Stay as long as possible. Note: do on one leg then on another.

4 - Lower Plank: 12 sec. Note: Keep your back straight and body tight.

1 - Tree Pose: Stay as long as possible. Note: do on one leg then on another.

5 - Book Pose: 15 sec. Note: Keep your core tight. Legs should be across from your eyes.

6 - Shavasana: 5 min. Note: this pose is very important and provides you with long term benefits. Try not to skip this. Close your eyes and imagine who you want to be and what your goals are! Always think happy thoughts.

Task: Color in the correct path to get to the bucket collecting leaves.

Keep at it!
This week we will learn about using commas, work with fractions and talk about respiration.

WEEK 5

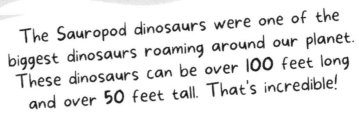

The Sauropod dinosaurs were one of the biggest dinosaurs roaming around our planet. These dinosaurs can be over **100** feet long and over **50** feet tall. That's incredible!

Basic Comma Use

Now that we're beginning to think about connecting ideas and crafting longer, more complex sentences, we also have to explore new ways to use **punctuation** to get our ideas across. One of your best friends when writing mature sentences is the **comma. Commas** provide important pauses for readers and break sentences up into smaller chunks, which makes them easier to analyze.

Today, we'll focus on the **three basic uses** of the comma. In a few weeks, we'll introduce some more advanced, exciting ones!

Commas in Lists
You <u>probably</u> already know about this use of the comma, but it's one of the most basic and important! When you make a **list** of objects, people, or adjectives, it's important to put a **comma** between each item.

The final item in a list usually has one of the coordinating conjunctions (and, but, or) before it. Some people like to include a comma (which is sometimes called the **Oxford Comma**) before those conjunctions. Other writers choose not to.

For Example...
- ✳ I went to the store and bought bananas, lettuce, mustard, and bread.
  - * The list uses the Oxford Comma (before "and")

- ✳ I went to the store and bought socks, shirts and a new pair of shoes.
  - * This list does not use the Oxford Comma (there's no comma before "and")

Using Commas to Separate an Introduction
Sometimes, an author wants to include a little introduction at the beginning of a sentence. Usually, those introductions contain context to help the reader understand where or when the events of the sentence happened.

For Example...
- ✳ After the movie, we went out to dinner.
  - * "After the movie" is an intro that helps the reader know when the speaker went to dinner.

- ✳ During winter, bears spend most of their time hibernating in dens.
  - * "During winter" is an into that helps the reader understand when bears spend most of their time hibernating.

Commas and Compound Sentences
A comma and a conjunction can be used together to connect two complete sentences. We'll talk about this more specifically next week!

For Example...
- ✳ Forming compound sentences is really important, but we're not going to dive too deep into it until next week.

From The Importance of Being Earnest

By Oscar Wilde

Algernon. How are you, my dear Ernest? What brings you up to town?

Jack. Oh, pleasure, pleasure! What else should bring one anywhere? Eating as usual, I see, Algy!

Algernon. [Stiffly.] I believe it is customary in good society to take some slight refreshment at five o'clock. Where have you been since last Thursday?

Jack. [Sitting down on the sofa.] In the country.

Algernon. What on earth do you do there?

Jack. [Pulling off his gloves.] When one is in town one amuses oneself. When one is in the country one amuses other people. It is excessively boring.

Algernon. And who are the people you amuse?

Jack. [Airily.] Oh, neighbours, neighbours.

Algernon. Got nice neighbours in your part of Shropshire?

Jack. Perfectly horrid! Never speak to one of them.

Algernon. How immensely you must amuse them! [Goes over and takes sandwich.] By the way, Shropshire is your county, is it not?

Jack. Eh? Shropshire? Yes, of course. Hallo! Why all these cups? Why cucumber sandwiches? Why such reckless extravagance in one so young? Who is coming to tea?

Algernon. Oh! merely Aunt Augusta and Gwendolen.

Jack. How perfectly delightful!

Algernon. Yes, that is all very well; but I am afraid Aunt Augusta won't quite approve of your being here.

Jack. May I ask why?

Algernon. My dear fellow, the way you flirt with Gwendolen is perfectly disgraceful. It is almost as bad as the way Gwendolen flirts with you.

Jack. I am in love with Gwendolen. I have come up to town expressly to propose to her.

Algernon. I thought you had come up for pleasure? . . . I call that business.

Jack. How utterly unromantic you are!

1. Why does Jack not like living in the **country?**

_____

_____

2. How does Jack know that Algernon is expecting **visitors?**

_____

_____

3. Which of these best describes the **tone** of this scene?

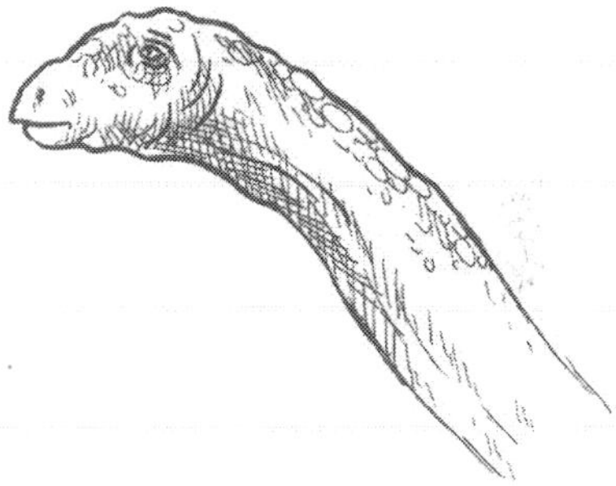

   A. Quirky and funny
   B. Dark and depressing
   C. Violent and disturbing
   D. Romantic and passionate

4. Which of these do we know is a main difference between **Jack** and **Algernon?**

   A. Jack is more outspoken and loud
   B. Algernon is more serious and dislikes humor
   C. Jack is more of a romantic
   D. Algernon is a loner, whereas Jack is more social

5. Based on the **tone** and **plot details** of what you've read, what do you predict will happen when Gwendolen and Aunt Augusta arrive?

_____

_____

_____

_____

_____

Inserting Commas as Needed

Directions: Read each sentence and, using your pen, write in commas wherever they are needed. (**Note:** a sentence may require more than one comma!)

1. Even though she normally didn't eat sweets Marilyn indulged in the chocolate cake.

2. Due to the decline in business the bookstore had to close permanently.

3. If you listen quietly you can hear the calls of several different kinds of birds.

4. Phil Bret Harrison Mike and Don are all going out for football this year.

5. Janice owns the school record for long jump but a lot of people think that LaToya will beat her this year.

Please be aware of your environment and be safe at all times. If you cannot do an exercise, just try your best.

Repeat these **exercises 4 ROUNDS**

2 - Lunges: 4 times to each leg.
Note: Use your body weight or books as weight to do leg lunges.

4 - Run: 50m
Note: Run 25 meters to one side and 25 meters back to the starting position.

1 - Abs: 15 times

3 - Plank: 20 sec.

From The Importance of Being Earnest

By Oscar Wilde

(Continued from Day One's Passage)
[Enter Lady Bracknell and Gwendolen.]

Lady Bracknell. Good afternoon, dear Algernon, I hope you are behaving very well.

Algernon. I'm feeling very well, Aunt Augusta.

Lady Bracknell. That's not quite the same thing. In fact the two things rarely go together. [Sees Jack and bows to him with icy coldness.]

Algernon. [To Gwendolen.] Dear me, you are smart!

Gwendolen. I am always smart! Am I not, Mr. Worthing?

Jack. You're quite perfect, Miss Fairfax.

Gwendolen. Oh! I hope I am not that. It would leave no room for developments, and I intend to develop in many directions. [Gwendolen and Jack sit down together in the corner.]

Lady Bracknell. I'm sorry if we are a little late, Algernon, but I was obliged to call on dear Lady Harbury. I hadn't been there since her poor husband's death. I never saw a woman so altered; she looks quite twenty years younger. And now I'll have a cup of tea, and one of those nice cucumber sandwiches you promised me.

Algernon. Certainly, Aunt Augusta. [Goes over to tea-table.]

Lady Bracknell. Won't you come and sit here, Gwendolen?

Gwendolen. Thanks, mamma, I'm quite comfortable where I am.

Algernon. [Picking up empty plate] Good heavens! Lane! Why are there no cucumber sandwiches? I ordered them specially.

Lane. [Gravely.] There were no cucumbers in the market this morning, sir. I went down twice.

Algernon. No cucumbers!

Lane. No, sir. Not even for ready money.

Algernon. That will do, Lane, thank you.

Lane. Thank you, sir. [Goes out.]

Algernon. I am greatly distressed, Aunt Augusta, about there being no cucumbers, not even for ready money.

1. Why does Lady Bracknell say there is a difference between **"behaving** very well" and **"feeling** very well?" What is she suggesting about Algernon?

_____

_____

2. Based on the passage, how would you describe Lady Bracknell's (also known as "Aunt Augusta" in Day One's passage) personality? What details helped you come to that conclusion?

_____

_____

3. What does Lady Bracknell **imply** about Lady Harbury?

   A. She is very distressed by her husband's death
   B. She is very plain and unattractive
   C. She is annoying and not a good friend
   D. She is happy her husband is dead

4. What is the purpose of the **second** comma in the sentence: "I'm sorry if we are a little late, Algernon, but I was obliged to call on dear Lady Harbury."

   A. To separate an introduction from the main body of a sentence
   B. The separate items in a list
   C. To create a compound sentence
   D. To give the reader a place to breathe.

5. Based on what you read in this passage **and** the content of Day One's passage, what statement by **Algernon** do we know is a **lie**?

_____

_____

_____

_____

_____

_____

Eliminating Unnecessary Commas

Directions: Each sentence below contains one comma that doesn't belong. Read carefully to figure out which comma is unnecessary, and circle it using your pen.

1. The American flag contains fifty stars, thirty stripes, and is red, white, and, blue.

2. In spite of the house's age, the roof was in great shape, so Mr. Daughtry decided to buy it, for his family.

3. During the fire drill, the confused, disoriented, students in Ms. Tracton's class went down the wrong staircase.

4. When people use commas to make lists, they have to decide, whether they want to use the Oxford Comma.

5. Our house is heated by a combination of fuels: oil, solar energy, and even, wood pellets.

FITNESS

Please be aware of your environment and be safe at all times. If you cannot do an exercise, just try your best.

Repeat these **exercises 4 ROUNDS**

2 - Side Bending: 10 times to each side. Note: try to touch your feet.

3 - Tree Pose: Stay as long as possible. Note: do the same with the other leg.

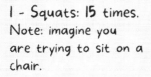

1 - Squats: 15 times. Note: imagine you are trying to sit on a chair.

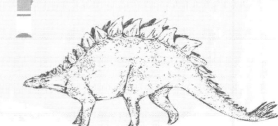

Interpreting fraction products

1. Find the product of $\frac{5}{6}$ and $\frac{4}{9}$.

   A. $\frac{9}{13}$

   B. $\frac{20}{13}$

   C. $\frac{20}{54}$

   D. $\frac{9}{54}$

2. Which expression is true?

   A. $\frac{6}{12} \times \frac{5}{12} = \frac{30}{12}$

   B. $3 \times \frac{7}{15} = \frac{3}{15} \times 7$

   C. $\frac{9}{14} \times \frac{3}{2} = \frac{12}{28}$

   D. $\frac{2}{5} \times \frac{5}{15} = \frac{9}{15}$

3. Choose a pair of fractions that result in a product of $\frac{21}{40}$.

   A. $\frac{7}{10}$ and $\frac{1}{4}$

   B. $\frac{15}{25}$ and $\frac{6}{15}$

   C. $\frac{7}{8}$ and $\frac{3}{20}$

   D. $\frac{3}{8}$ and $\frac{7}{5}$

4. What is the missing fraction in the equation ____ $\times \frac{4}{16} = \frac{64}{32}$?

   A. $\frac{8}{2}$

   B. $\frac{16}{2}$

   C. $\frac{60}{16}$

   D. $8\frac{1}{2}$

5. What is the product of $\frac{8}{18} \times \frac{5}{6}$?

   A. $\frac{40}{108}$

   B. $\frac{13}{24}$

   C. $\frac{13}{108}$

   D. $\frac{40}{18}$

6. You can get the number **2** by multiplying $\frac{3}{6}$ by the number ____.

   A. $\frac{12}{4}$ C. $\frac{8}{2}$

   B. $\frac{4}{2}$ D. $\frac{8}{12}$

7. Determine the fraction that correctly fills in the blank. $\frac{3}{5} \times$ ____ $= \frac{27}{35}$.

   A. $\frac{24}{30}$ C. $\frac{7}{9}$

   B. $\frac{9}{35}$ D. $\frac{9}{7}$

DIPLODOCUS

90

8. Find the product of $\frac{12}{14}$ and $\frac{6}{8}$.

   A. $\frac{72}{112}$

   B. $\frac{18}{22}$

   C. $\frac{18}{112}$

   D. $\frac{72}{22}$

9. The fraction $\frac{36}{45}$ can be found by multiplying $\frac{2}{5}$ by the number _____.

   A. $\frac{9}{18}$

   B. $\frac{34}{40}$

   C. $\frac{18}{9}$

   D. $\frac{18}{45}$

10. Which expression is FALSE?

   A. $\frac{6}{14} \times 5 = 6 \times \frac{5}{14}$

   B. $\frac{4}{2} \times \frac{8}{16} = 1$

   C. $\frac{7}{21} \times \frac{5}{8} = \frac{7 \times 5}{21 \times 8}$

   D. $2\frac{1}{4} \times 3 = 6\frac{1}{4}$

11. What is $\frac{25}{32} \times \frac{2}{3}$?

_____

12. Solve the problem $5\frac{3}{8} \times 2$.

_____

13. Find the product of $2\frac{2}{3}$ and $1\frac{1}{5}$.

_____

FITNESS

Please be aware of your environment and be safe at all times. If you cannot do an exercise, just try your best.

Repeat these **exercises 4 ROUNDS**

1 - Bend forward: 15 times.
Note: try to touch your feet. Make sure to keep your back straight and if needed you can bend your knees.

2 - Lunges: 7 times to each leg.
Note: Use your body weight or books as weight to do leg lunges.

4 - Abs: 15 times

3 - Plank: 20 sec.

Finding the area of a rectangle with fractional side lengths

1. What is the area of the rectangle with two sides of $\frac{6}{10}$ inches long and two sides of $\frac{2}{5}$ inches long?

   A. $\frac{12}{50}$ sq in

   B. $\frac{8}{50}$ sq in

   C. $\frac{8}{15}$ sq in

   D. 15 sq in

2. What is the area of the rectangle?

   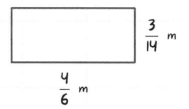

   $\frac{3}{14}$ m

   $\frac{4}{6}$ m

   A. $\frac{7}{20}$ sq m

   B. $\frac{12}{20}$ sq m

   C. $\frac{12}{84}$ sq m

   D. $\frac{7}{84}$ sq m

3. The perimeter of a square is $\frac{4}{9}$ feet. What is the area of the square?

   A. $\frac{16}{9}$ sq ft

   B. $\frac{1}{81}$ sq ft

   C. $\frac{16}{81}$ sq ft

   D. $\frac{1}{36}$ sq ft

4. Find the area of the rectangle below.

   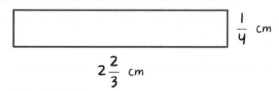

   $\frac{1}{4}$ cm

   $2\frac{2}{3}$ cm

   A. $\frac{8}{12}$ sq cm

   C. $4\frac{3}{12}$ sq cm

   B. $4\frac{2}{12}$ sq cm

   D. $2\frac{1}{12}$ sq cm

5. What is the area of the rectangle shown below?

   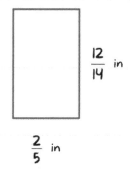

   $\frac{12}{14}$ in

   $\frac{2}{5}$ in

   A. $\frac{14}{19}$ sq in

   C. $\frac{14}{70}$ sq in

   B. $\frac{24}{19}$ sq in

   D. $\frac{24}{70}$ sq in

6. The shaded part of the square below has a length of $\frac{7}{9}$ in and a width of $\frac{2}{3}$ in.

   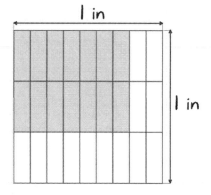

   1 in

   1 in

What is the area of the shaded part of the square in square inches?

A. $\frac{7}{27}$ sq in   C. $\frac{2}{27}$ sq in

B. $\frac{14}{27}$ sq in   D. $\frac{7}{14}$ sq in

7. The shaded part of the square below has a length of $\frac{6}{8}$ centimeters and a width of $\frac{4}{9}$ centimeters.

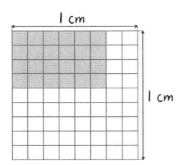

What is the area of the shaded part of the square in square centimeters?

A. $\frac{10}{17}$ sq cm   C. $\frac{10}{81}$ sq cm

B. $\frac{24}{17}$ sq cm   D. $\frac{24}{72}$ sq cm

8. What is the area of the rectangle with two sides of $2\frac{1}{4}$ inches long and two sides of $\frac{3}{8}$ inches wide?

A. $2\frac{4}{12}$ sq in   C. $\frac{27}{32}$ sq in

B. $2\frac{3}{24}$ sq in   D. $\frac{27}{8}$ sq in

9. Find the area of the rectangle below.

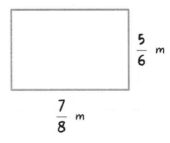

A. $\frac{12}{14}$ sq m   C. $\frac{35}{14}$ sq m

B. $\frac{35}{48}$ sq m   D. $\frac{12}{48}$ sq m

FITNESS

Please be aware of your environment and be safe at all times. If you cannot do an exercise, just try your best.

Repeat these **exercises 4 ROUNDS**

1 - High Plank: 20 sec.

2 - Chair: 15 sec.
Note: sit on an imaginary chair, keep your back straight.

3 - Waist Hooping: 15 times. Note: if you do not have a hoop, pretend you have an imaginary hoop and rotate your hips 10 times.

4 - Abs: 15 times

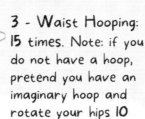

Problems with fractions and multiplication

1. What is $\frac{3}{8} \times 4$?

   A. $\frac{12}{32}$ C. $1\frac{3}{8}$

   B. $1\frac{1}{2}$ D. $\frac{10}{8}$

2. Determine which of the following answer choices shown below is less than 1.

   A. $\frac{10}{8}$ C. $4 \times \frac{2}{9}$

   B. $5 \times \frac{1}{2}$ D. $2 \times \frac{1}{2}$

3. Solve the problem $3\frac{1}{6} \times 2$.

   A. $3\frac{2}{6}$

   B. $6\frac{1}{6}$

   C. $6\frac{2}{12}$

   D. $6\frac{2}{6}$

4. The product of $\frac{3}{5} \times 2$ is:

   A. Less than 1
   B. Equal to 1
   C. Greater than 1
   D. None of the above

5. What is $3\frac{4}{5} \times 5$?

   A. 35
   B. 19
   C. 60
   D. 12

6. Which expression is true?

   A. $4 \times \frac{1}{2} < 1$

   B. $\frac{4}{2} \times \frac{6}{6} = 2$

   C. $3\frac{7}{9} \times 9 = 37$

   D. $\frac{2}{3} \times \frac{5}{2} < 1$

7. Determine which of the following answer choices shown below is greater than 1.

   A. $\frac{1}{6} \times \frac{6}{4}$

   B. $3 \times \frac{3}{12}$

   C. $1 \times \frac{2}{5}$

   D. $\frac{2}{8} \times 5$

8. Which expression is FALSE?

   A. $6 \times \frac{3}{5} < 1$

   B. $\frac{3}{12} \times 4 = 1$

   C. $\frac{6}{8} \times \frac{3}{3} = \frac{3}{4}$

   D. $\frac{5}{9} \times \frac{7}{3} > 1$

9. The product of $\frac{3}{7} \times 2$ is:

   A. Less than 1
   B. Equal to 1
   C. Greater than 1
   D. None of the above

10. What is $6\frac{1}{4} \times 3$?

    A. $6\frac{3}{4}$ C. $18\frac{3}{4}$

    B. $6\frac{3}{12}$ D. $18\frac{3}{4}$

11. Determine which of the following answer choices shown below is equal to 1.

    A. $4 \times \frac{2}{12}$ C. $2 \times \frac{6}{3}$

    B. $3 \times \frac{3}{6}$ D. $6 \times \frac{8}{48}$

12. The product of $2\frac{3}{5} \times \frac{1}{3}$ is:

    A. Less than 1

    B. Equal to 1

    C. Greater than 1

    D. None of the above

13. Solve the problem $5\frac{3}{8} \times 4$.

14. What is $\frac{5}{6} \times 2$?

15. Which number would complete the equation $\frac{6}{2} \times \frac{?}{5} = 3$?

16. Determine if the product of $\frac{3}{14} \times 6$ is 'less than', 'equal to', or 'greater than' 1.

17. Which number would complete the equation $\frac{5}{15} \times \frac{?}{2} = 1$?

18. Solve the problem $6\frac{5}{20} \times 5$.

YOGA

Please be aware of your environment and be safe at all times. If you cannot do an exercise, just try your best.

1 - Down Dog: 25 sec.

2 - Bend Down: 25 sec.

3 - Chair: 20 sec.

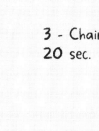

4 - Child Pose: 25 sec.

5 - Shavasana: as long as you can. Note: think of happy moments and relax your mind.

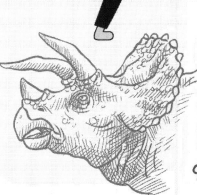

Observing Respiration

All living organisms on Earth need oxygen to live and function. Every person, plant, animal, and cell gets the **oxygen** it needs and expels the waste gas **carbon dioxide** through a process known as **respiration**. Today, we'll observe how even the tiniest microorganisms absorb air and release carbon dioxide, just like we do when we breathe.

Materials:

* I empty plastic bottle, about **20** oz. (Clear plastic will be best for your observations)
* I rubber balloon (uninflated)
* Warm running water
* Measuring spoons
* A long spoon or stick (for stirring)
* A packet of fast-acting dried yeast (available in the baking aisle of the supermarket)
* Sugar (just one teaspoon will do)
* Notepaper
* A timer
* A ruler or tape measure

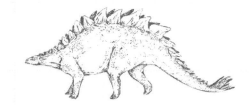

Procedure:

1. Make sure your empty plastic bottle is completely clean and dry.

2. Stretch the neck of the balloon a few times and blow it up at least half-way once or twice using your mouth. This will ensure it's not too stiff to inflate later. **Do not** tie the end of the balloon shut; just let it deflate. (**Note:** If you feel uncomfortable pressure in your ears as you blow up the balloon, ask an adult to help you.)

3. Pour about an **inch** of warm water (not hot) into the bottom of your plastic bottle.

4. Open the packet of yeast, dump it into the water at the bottom of the bottle, and stir the mixture with your stick or spoon until everything is evenly incorporated.

5. Using your measuring spoons, add one teaspoon of sugar to the mixture of yeast and warm water. Stir it in as well.

6. Stretch the mouth of the balloon over the top of the plastic bottle so it is tightly sealed. It should look like your bottle is wearing a little hat.

7. Set your timer for **30** minutes and check in on your bottle **at least every five minutes** during that span. Each time, write down some observations of what you're seeing in the clear plastic bottle as well as the balloon. If you want, you can even carefully measure the balloon using a ruler or tape measure each time and mark down how big it gets in your notes.

8. After **30** minutes, make your final measurements and observations. If the balloon had a good seal, it should be at least somewhat inflated due to the respiration of the tiny organisms in the yeast. The mixture of warm water and sugar woke up those dried out, sleeping organisms, and they went to work **consuming oxygen** and sugar and **creating carbon dioxide** – just like we do when we breathe. If you want, you can remove the balloon and make final observations of the yeast mixture in the bottle.

9. Make sure to dispose of your materials properly. The yeast mixture in the bottle can get a little smelly if you leave it sitting around for too long.

Follow-Up Questions:

1. Did your balloon grow at a **steady rate**, or was there a certain point in the process where the yeast seemed to do the majority of its work? What do your **notes** tell you about the progress of the yeast?

_____

_____

2. Based on what you saw, why do you think yeast is important to making bread? What might bread without **yeast** be like?

_____

YOGA

Please be aware of your environment and be safe at all times. If you cannot do an exercise, just try your best.

2 - Down Dog: 25 sec.

3 - Stretching: Stay as long as possible. Note: do on one leg then on another.

4 - Lower Plank: 12 sec. Note: Keep your back straight and body tight.

1 - Tree Pose: Stay as long as possible. Note: do on one leg then on another.

5 - Book Pose: 15 sec. Note: Keep your core tight. Legs should be across from your eyes.

6 - Shavasana: 5 min. Note: this pose is very important and provides you with long term benefits. Try not to skip this. Close your eyes and imagine who you want to be and what your goals are! Always think happy thoughts.

Task: There are four ropes below. One person is holding one end of the rope and another person is holding the other end of the rope. Find out the matching pairs of people holding the same rope.

Are you having fun learning new concepts? Learning should always be fun! We tend to remember more information when we enjoy the learning experience.

WEEK 6

Some species of dinosaurs were carnivores, meat-eaters. Other dinosaurs were herbivores, plant-eaters. Only a few species were omnivores who ate both meat and plants.

Compound Sentences

Last week, we introduced the idea of using commas to break up sentences into more digestible chunks. We explored how to format a list (with or without the Oxford Comma) and also examined how to separate an introduction from the main body of the sentence. We said we'd wait to talk fully about compound sentences, though – so now it's time to do that!

Compound sentences are combinations of related sentences. They can be highly effective for showing when two ideas are closely connected. However, you must put commas in the correct places (and leave them out of the wrong places) in order to create a strong compound sentence.

Key Terms

Compound Sentence: A sentence made out of two complete, grammatically correct sentences, which are connected using a comma and a conjunction.

For Example...

- **Sentence 1:** I thought driving a car would be easy.
- **Sentence 2:** Driving a car is actually very difficult.
- **Conjunction:** But (because Sentence 2 is **disagreeing** with the ideas from Sentence 1)
- **Compound Sentence:** I thought driving a car would be easy, but it is actually very difficult.

- **Sentence 1:** The Smiths had a great vacation in Vermont.
- **Sentence 2:** The Smiths are planning on going to Vermont again next year.
- **Conjunction:** And (because Sentence 2 is **reinforcing or agreeing** with the ideas from Sentence 1)
- **Compound Sentence:** The Smiths had a great vacation in Vermont, and they're planning on returning next year.

Hint:

Before you insert a comma, make sure you're actually **connecting two sentences**. If you're just connecting **different parts of the subject** or **different parts of the predicate,** you don't need a comma!

For Example...

- Mikey and Crystal are best friends and neighbors.
    * You **don't** need to put any commas in this sentence because "Mikey and Crystal" are both parts of the **complete subject**. Also "friends and neighbors" are both parts of the **complete predicate**.
    * Remember, it's only a **compound sentence** if you're connecting **two complete sentences - not just words or ideas!**

From "The Secret Agent"

By Joseph Conrad

Mr Verloc, going out in the morning, left his shop nominally in charge of his brother-in-law. It could be done, because there was very little business at any time, and practically none at all before the evening. Mr Verloc cared but little about his ostensible business. And, moreover, his wife was in charge of his brother-in-law.

The shop was small, and so was the house. It was one of those grimy brick houses which existed in large quantities before the era of reconstruction dawned upon London. The shop was a square box of a place, with the front glazed in small panes. In the daytime the door remained closed; in the evening it stood discreetly but suspiciously ajar.

The window contained photographs of dancing girls; nondescript packages in wrappers like patent medicines; closed yellow paper envelopes, very flimsy, and marked two-and-six in heavy black figures; a few numbers of ancient French comic publications hung across a string as if to dry; a dingy blue china bowl, a casket of black wood, bottles of marking ink, and rubber stamps; a few books, with titles hinting at impropriety; a few apparently old copies of obscure newspapers, badly printed, with titles like The Torch, The Gong—rousing titles. And the two gas jets inside the panes were always turned low, either for economy's sake or for the sake of the customers.

These customers were either very young men, who hung about the window for a time before slipping in suddenly; or men of a more mature age, but looking generally as if they were not in funds. Some of that last kind had the collars of their overcoats turned right up to their moustaches, and traces of mud on the bottom of their nether garments, which had the appearance of being much worn and not very valuable. And the legs inside them did not, as a general rule, seem of much account either. With their hands plunged deep in the side pockets of their coats, they dodged in sideways, one shoulder first, as if afraid to start the bell going.

The bell, hung on the door by means of a curved ribbon of steel, was difficult to circumvent. It was hopelessly cracked; but of an evening, at the slightest provocation, it clattered behind the customer with impudent virulence.

1. Why is Mr. Verloc comfortable leaving his brother-in-law in charge of his shop?

    _____

    _____

2. How would you describe the **setting** of this scene in your own words?

    _____

    _____

3. Which of these is a **compound sentence?**

    A. Mr. Verloc cared but little about his ostensible business. (Paragraph 1)
    B. And, moreover, his wife was in charge of his brother-in-law. (Paragraph 1)
    C. The shop was small, and so was the house. (Paragraph 2)
    D. It was one of those grimy brick houses which existed in large quantities before the era of reconstruction dawned upon London. (Paragraph 2)

4. What aspect of the men who come to Mr. Verloc's shop matches with the title "The Secret Agent?"

    A. All of them are spies
    B. All of them seem very suspicious and secretive
    C. All of them appear to be poor
    D. All of them want to avoid setting off the bell

    CRONOSAURUS

5. Based on the title and the events of this passage, what do you **predict** is going to happen to Mr. Verloc?

    _____

    _____

    _____

    _____

    _____

Completing the Compound Sentence

Directions: Each compound sentence below is missing its comma! Read each sentence, then insert commas with your pencil or pen where they are needed. **(Note: These commas could be part of a list, an introduction, or a compound sentence.)**

1. Cutler Automotive and Bryce Group are merging this winter and that new company will be the largest used car dealer in the state.

2. Susan Kraft has been my secretary for fifteen years and during that time she has never missed a single day of work.

3. Piper Allie and Marjory are in charge of designing the costumes for the play but Ms. Frankel is technically supervising them.

4. Neither Mr. Hank nor Ms. Parker have ever read a comic book and I want to open their eyes to the endless worlds of heroes villains and adventure.

5. Most days I eat lunch in the cafeteria or if I'm behind on my work Ms. Partridge lets me eat in her classroom while I do math.

FITNESS

Please be aware of your environment and be safe at all times. If you cannot do an exercise, just try your best.

Repeat these **exercises 4 ROUNDS**

2 - Lunges: 4 times to each leg.
Note: Use your body weight or books as weight to do leg lunges.

4 - Run: 50m
Note: Run 25 meters to one side and 25 meters back to the starting position.

1 - Abs: 15 times

3 - Plank: 20 sec.

From "The Secret Agent"

By Joseph Conrad

Such was the house, the household, and the business Mr Verloc left behind him on his way westward at the hour of half-past ten in the morning. It was unusually early for him; his whole person exhaled the charm of almost dewy freshness; he wore his blue cloth overcoat unbuttoned; his boots were shiny; his cheeks, freshly shaven, had a sort of gloss; and even his heavy-lidded eyes, refreshed by a night of peaceful slumber, sent out glances of comparative alertness.

Through the park railings these glances beheld men and women riding in the Row, couples cantering past harmoniously, others advancing sedately at a walk, loitering groups of three or four, solitary horsemen looking unsociable, and solitary women followed at a long distance by a groom with a cockade to his hat and a leather belt over his tight-fitting coat. Carriages went bowling by, mostly two-horse broughams, with here and there a victoria with the skin of some wild beast inside and a woman's face and hat emerging above the folded hood.

And a peculiarly London sun—against which nothing could be said except that it looked bloodshot—glorified all this by its stare. It hung at a moderate elevation above Hyde Park Corner with an air of punctual and benign vigilance. The very pavement under Mr Verloc's feet had an old-gold tinge in that diffused light, in which neither wall, nor tree, nor beast, nor man cast a shadow. Mr Verloc was going westward through a town without shadows in an atmosphere of powdered old gold. There were red, coppery gleams on the roofs of houses, on the corners of walls, on the panels of carriages, on the very coats of the horses, and on the broad back of Mr Verloc's overcoat, where they produced a dull effect of rustiness. But Mr Verloc was not in the least conscious of having got rusty. He surveyed through the park railings the evidences of the town's opulence and luxury with an approving eye.

All these people had to be protected. Protection is the first necessity of opulence and luxury. They had to be protected; and their horses, carriages, houses, servants had to be protected; and the source of their wealth had to be protected in the heart of the city and the heart of the country; the whole social order favourable to their hygienic idleness had to be protected against the shallow enviousness of unhygienic labour.

1. Based on the passage, how would you describe Mr. Verloc's personality?

    _____

    _____

2. How would you describe the setting that Mr. Verloc is describing in the passage?

    _____

    _____

3. Why are things described as looking like "gold" throughout Paragraph 3?

    A. Because of the uncharacteristic brightness of the sun
    B. Because everybody is very rich in this part of town
    C. To show that Mr. Verloc only cares about money
    D. To show that London is the perfect city

4. What does the narrator suggest that Mr. Verloc believes at the end of the passage?

    A. That people do not deserve protection
    B. That the rich are lazy
    C. That the city is too dirty
    D. That rich people's servants deserve protection more than the rich themselves

5. How does the author show that Mr. Verloc sees the world differently from the way most other people do?

    _____

    _____

    _____

    _____

    _____

Creating a Compound Sentence

Directions: Read each group of sentences. Then, decide which conjunction could be used to connect them effectively and write your new compound sentence on the lines below. Remember to think about ways to minimize repetitive wording in your compound sentences - you don't want to be repeating words over and over again when you don't need to.

1.

- o **Sentence 1:** Poisonous snakes can be highly dangerous for hikers.
- o **Sentence 2:** There are no poisonous snakes in this part of the state.
- o **Conjunction:** _____
- o **Compound Sentence:** _____

_____

_____

2.

- o **Sentence 1:** You can write your answers on the math test in the form of fractions.
- o **Sentence 2:** You can write your answers on the math test in the form of percentages.
- o **Conjunction:** _____
- o **Compound Sentence:** _____

_____

_____

3.

- o **Sentence 1:** There is going to be a demolition derby at the town fair.
- o **Sentence 2:** Everybody is excited to see the crazy spectacle at the town fair.
- o **Conjunction:** _____
- o **Compound Sentence:** _____

_____

FITNESS

Please be aware of your environment and be safe at all times. If you cannot do an exercise, just try your best.

Repeat these **exercises 4 ROUNDS**

1 - Squats: 15 times. Note: imagine you are trying to sit on a chair.

2 - Side Bending: 10 times to each side. Note: try to touch your feet.

3 - Tree Pose: Stay as long as possible. Note: do the same with the other leg.

WEEK 6
DAY 3   MATH

Real world problems multiply/ divide fractions

1. Henry spends $ $25\frac{3}{4}$ on food every week. How much does he spend on food in 8 weeks?

   A. $200
   B. $202
   C. $204
   D. $206

2. Ann swims $\frac{3}{12}$ of a mile per day. How many miles does she swim in 7 days?

3. There are $4\frac{2}{7}$ pounds of potatoes in one box. How many pounds of potatoes are there in 5 boxes?

   A. $4\frac{10}{35}$ pounds
   B. $20\frac{10}{35}$ pounds
   C. $21\frac{3}{7}$ pounds
   D. $21\frac{3}{35}$ pounds

4. Sophia practiced her violin for $3\frac{3}{5}$ hours. Benjamin practiced 3 times that long. Which equation could be used to find how long Benjamin practiced?

   A. $3\frac{3}{5} \times \frac{1}{3} = 3\frac{4}{8}$
   B. $3\frac{3}{5} \times \frac{1}{3} = 3\frac{3}{15}$
   C. $3\frac{3}{5} \times 3 = 10\frac{4}{5}$
   D. $3\frac{3}{5} \times 3 = 9\frac{9}{15}$

5. Jane had a ribbon that was $4\frac{1}{3}$ feet long. If she buys another ribbon $1\frac{1}{2}$ times longer than her current ribbon, how long would they be together?

   A. $6\frac{1}{2}$ ft   C. $4\frac{1}{6}$ ft
   B. $4\frac{2}{5}$ ft   D. $10\frac{5}{6}$ ft

6. A math lesson was $1\frac{2}{5}$ hours long. The English lesson was only $\frac{2}{6}$ as long. How many hours long was the English lesson?

   A. $1\frac{4}{11}$ C. $\frac{14}{\frac{11}{15}}$
   B. $1\frac{4}{30}$ D.

7. Mr. Joel spent $2\frac{3}{8}$ hours fixing his car. Rick spent 3 times as long as Mr. Joel to fix his car. How much time did Rick spend on fixing the car?

8. There were $14\frac{8}{12}$ pounds of pineapples in each box. How many pounds of pineapples were there in 6 boxes?

9. Mike practiced his piano for $\frac{5}{6}$ of an hour. How many minutes did he practice?

    A. 42 minutes
    B. 48 minutes
    C. 50 minutes
    D. 55 minutes

10. Daniel practiced math problems $2\frac{2}{6}$ hours on Monday. On Tuesday he practiced $\frac{3}{5}$ as long. Which equation could be used to find how many hours Daniel practiced on Tuesday?

    A. $2\frac{2}{6} \times \frac{5}{3} = 2\frac{10}{18}$

    B. $2\frac{2}{6} \times \frac{3}{5} = 1\frac{2}{5}$

    C. $2\frac{2}{6} \times \frac{3}{5} = 2\frac{10}{30}$

    D. $2\frac{2}{6} \times \frac{5}{3} = 1\frac{1}{3}$

11. Mary had $2\frac{5}{9}$ pounds of apples. Her mother bought 7 times as many as Mary had. How many pounds of apples do they have together?

FITNESS

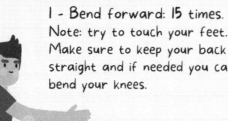

Please be aware of your environment and be safe at all times. If you cannot do an exercise, just try your best.

1 - Bend forward: 15 times. Note: try to touch your feet. Make sure to keep your back straight and if needed you can bend your knees.

2 - Lunges: 7 times to each leg. Note: Use your body weight or books as weight to do leg lunges.

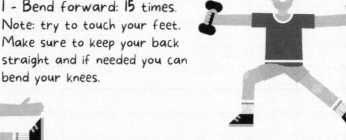

3 - Plank: 20 sec.

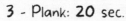

4 - Abs: 15 times

Repeat these
exercises
4 ROUNDS

Rounding numbers to thousands, hundreds, tens, ones, tenths, hundredths, and thousandths place

1. What is 65,973 rounded to the nearest thousand?

    A. 65,900
    B. 65,000
    C. 66,000
    D. 70,000

2. Choose the number which after rounding to the nearest hundred becomes less.

    A. 67,358
    C. 14,151
    B. 23,929
    D. 55,671

3. Round 27.965 to the tenths place.

    A. 27.9
    C. 28
    B. 27.97
    D. 30

4. What is 108.326 rounded to hundredths place?

    A. 108.32
    C. 108.3
    B. 108.33
    D. 100

5. Which of the following numbers rounded to the nearest hundred gives you 6,100?

    A. 6,145
    C. 6,154
    B. 6,039
    D. 6,205

6. What is 984,754 rounded to the nearest thousand?

    A. 984,700
    C. 984,000
    B. 984,800
    D. 985,000

7. Choose the number which after rounding to the hundredths place becomes greater.

    A. 8.974
    C. 0.945
    B. 7.163
    D. 6.121

8. Which decimal is greater rounded to the nearest thousandths?

    A. 9.7823
    C. 6.0302
    B. 7.6455
    D. 4.7361

9. Which of the following numbers rounded to the nearest hundredths gives you 45.9?

    A. 45.938
    C. 45.896
    B. 45.922
    D. 45.908

10. Round 65.934 to the tenths place.

    A. 65.93
    B. 65.9
    C. 66
    D. 70

11. Which of the following numbers rounded to the nearest hundredths gives you 1?

    A. 0.993
    B. 0.995
    C. 1.096
    D. 1.009

12. Round 876.355 to the nearest hundredths.

    A. 880
    B. 900
    C. 876.36
    D. 876.4

13. Round 236.987 to the nearest tens.

    _____

14. Which place value should you round in 5,472 to get 5,000?

15. What is 8.367 rounded to the nearest tenths?

16. Which place value should you round in 7.349 to get 7.35?

17. Round 65.8763 to the nearest thousandths.

18. Round 8,460.127 to the nearest thousand.

19. Round 7.346 and 7.342 to the nearest hundredths. Write a number sentence using those two rounded numbers and a comparison symbol.

20. What is 6.995 rounded to the nearest hundredths?

FITNESS

Please be aware of your environment and be safe at all times. If you cannot do an exercise, just try your best.

1 - High Plank: 20 sec.

2 - Chair: 15 sec.
Note: sit on an imaginary chair, keep your back straight.

4 - Abs: 15 times

3 - Waist Hooping: 15 times. Note: if you do not have a hoop, pretend you have an imaginary hoop and rotate your hips 10 times.

Repeat these **exercises 4 ROUNDS**

Area & Perimeter

1. What is the area of the rectangle?

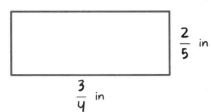

$\frac{2}{5}$ in

$\frac{3}{4}$ in

A. $\frac{3}{10}$ sq in

C. $\frac{15}{8}$ sq in

B. $\frac{5}{9}$ sq in

D. $1\frac{3}{5}$ sq in

2. Find the perimeter of the shape.

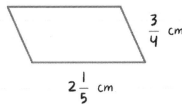

$\frac{3}{4}$ cm

$2\frac{1}{5}$ cm

A. $4\frac{6}{8}$ cm

B. $4\frac{4}{9}$ cm

C. $5\frac{9}{10}$ cm

D. $5\frac{4}{20}$ cm

3. Find the area of the triangle shown below.

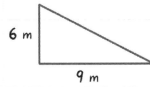

6 m

9 m

A. 54 sq m
B. 27 sq m
C. 30 sq m
D. 15 sq m

4. The perimeter of the square is $6\frac{4}{16}$ centimeters. What is the area of the square?

A. $\frac{625}{256}$ sq cm

C. $40\frac{1}{16}$ sq cm

B. $3\frac{1}{16}$ sq cm

D. $36\frac{1}{16}$ sq cm

5. Find the perimeter of the triangle below.

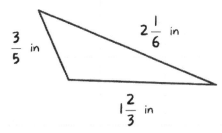

$\frac{3}{5}$ in

$2\frac{1}{6}$ in

$1\frac{2}{3}$ in

A. $3\frac{6}{14}$ in

C. $4\frac{13}{30}$ in

B. $3\frac{5}{6}$ in

D. $4\frac{1}{15}$ in

6. The perimeter of the rectangle is $\frac{4}{6}$ yards and the length is $\frac{1}{4}$ yards. What is the area of the rectangle?

A. $\frac{1}{6}$ sq yd

C. $\frac{1}{24}$ sq yd

B. $\frac{1}{8}$ sq yd

D. $\frac{1}{48}$ sq yd

7. Find the area of the shaded part below.

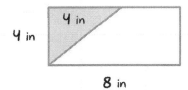

4 in

4 in

8 in

A. 32 sq in
B. 16 sq in
C. 12 sq in
D. 8 sq in

8. The perimeter of the square is 96 feet. What is the area of the shaded part?

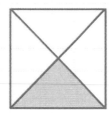

A. 96 sq ft
B. 112 sq ft
C. 144 sq ft
D. 156 sq ft

9. Find the area of the shape below.

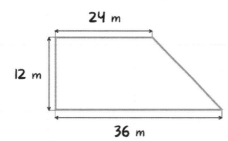

24 m

12 m

36 m

A. 240 sq m
B. 360 sq m
C. 480 sq m
D. 520 sq m

10. What is the area and perimeter of this rectangle?

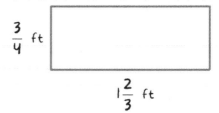

$\frac{3}{4}$ ft

$1\frac{2}{3}$ ft

11. Find the area of the triangle.

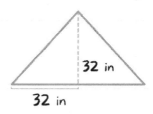

32 in

32 in

A. 512 sq in
B. 1,024 sq in
C. 768 sq in
D. 2,048 sq in

YOGA

Please be aware of your environment and be safe at all times. If you cannot do an exercise, just try your best.

1 - Down Dog: 25 sec.

2 - Bend Down: 25 sec.

3 - Chair: 20 sec.

4 - Child Pose: 25 sec.

5 - Shavasana: as long as you can. Note: think of happy moments and relax your mind.

EXPERIMENT

Understanding How We Breathe

Last week, we used yeast to show that all, even the smallest, living organisms **respire**. That is just a fancy way of saying they absorb oxygen from the environment, use it to power their bodies, and then emit the waste gas carbon dioxide. Of course, our big, complex human bodies handle respiration in a much different way from the yeast we looked at.

This time, we're going to create a model to help us understand how our lungs work, just like we did with our heart in *Week 4!*

Materials:

* An empty, clean, dry 2-liter bottle
* A kitchen trash bag
* A rubber balloon (uninflated)
* Masking tape
* Scissors
* A strong, thick rubber band
* Some sort of clay, putty, or dough (to form a tight seal)
* A drinking straw

Procedure:

1. Using a sharp pair of scissors **and help from an adult,** cut the top half off the two-liter bottle so you have the neck of the bottle and about four inches of plastic below it.

2. Using your scissors, cut a square of plastic out of your kitchen bag that is big enough to lay across the wide cut side of the half-bottle. Your plastic sheet should be a little bigger than the lip of the bottle, so it can be secured effectively.

3. Stretch your rubber band around the wide lip of the cut bottle to secure the plastic. The plastic sheet should be tight like a drum skin. You can trim excess plastic afterward using scissors.

4. Place one end of your drinking straw into the uninflated balloon. Then, wrap some tape tightly around the neck of the balloon so that the straw is pinched in there and you can inflate the balloon by blowing into the straw.

5. Place your half-bottle on the table with the plastic sheet on the bottom so the original neck/mouth of the bottle is facing upward. Carefully lower the balloon into the bottle using your straw, then seal the straw into the neck of the bottle using your clay, putty, or dough.

6. Take a four inch piece of masking tape and fold it sticky side to sticky side for about 75% of its length, creating a handle with two sticky tabs.

7. Attach the stick tabs of your tape handle to the bottom of the plastic sheet.

8. Gently tug on the tape handle you've just made and observe what happens to the balloon inside the bottle as you pull the plastic sheet away and let go of it. That plastic represents your **diaphragm**, a strong muscle that fires to tell your lungs to fill and empty. The balloon represents a lung, filling and emptying on command, and the straw is your windpipe, which connects your lungs and the outside world.

Follow-Up Questions:

1. Based on what you saw, how could a problem with the **diaphragm** result in trouble breathing?

_____

_____

_____

2. What do you think would happen if there was a hole in the **balloon**? How does that connect to the idea of your lungs?

_____

_____

_____

YOGA

Please be aware of your environment and be safe at all times. If you cannot do an exercise, just try your best.

1 - Tree Pose: Stay as long as possible. Note: do on one leg then on another.

2 - Down Dog: 25 sec.

3 - Stretching: Stay as long as possible. Note: do on one leg then on another.

4 - Lower Plank: 12 sec. Note: Keep your back straight and body tight.

5 - Book Pose: 15 sec. Note: Keep your core tight. Legs should be across from your eyes.

6 - Shavasana: 5 min. Note: this pose is very important and provides you with long term benefits. Try not to skip this. Close your eyes and imagine who you want to be and what your goals are! Always think happy thoughts.

Task: Locate the correct headphone that is plugged into the music player.

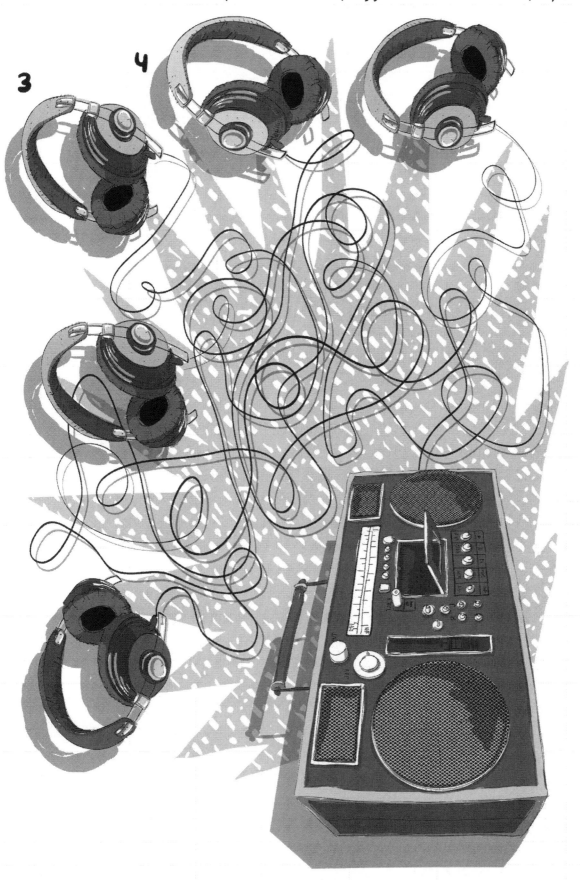

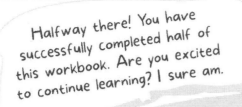

Halfway there! You have successfully completed half of this workbook. Are you excited to continue learning? I sure am.

WEEK 7

The oldest dinosaur that we know of is the Eoraptor that lived over **228** million years ago! These were small creatures that ate meat and weighed about **25** pounds.

Intermediate Comma Use

You're already familiar with using commas for lists, introductions, and compound sentences, but there's another really important use of the comma we haven't talked about yet: separating **nonessential modifiers** from the body of a sentence.

Nonessential modifiers are basically **bonus information** that give the reader more detail and better insight into your sentence but aren't fundamental to the sentence being correct. That means that if you **removed** a nonessential modifier from the sentence, that sentence would still make sense and have almost exactly the same meaning.

Key Terms

Nonessential Modifier: A phrase in the middle or at the end of a sentence that provides additional detail for the reader

So, what role do commas play?

Authors separate nonessential modifiers from the main body of their sentences using **commas!** We've already seen one specific example of this: The introduction.

* **After the ballgame,** we drove back home.
    * The introduction **After the ballgame** is basically a piece of bonus information that gives the reader context and helps them understand when and from where the people in the sentence drove back home.
    * The main body of the sentence "We drove back home" still makes perfect sense without the modifier, which tells us it's nonessential.

If a nonessential modifier containing bonus information comes at the **end** of a sentence, it should be separated from the body of the sentence with a comma.

* I drive a silver pickup truck, **which I bought five years ago.**
    * "Which I bought five years ago" provides the reader with **bonus information** about the truck, but it doesn't affect the meaning of the body of the sentence "I drive a silver truck." That tells us it's nonessential!

* Anthony went to the airport to pick up his grandmother, **who was flying in from Minnesota.**
    * "Who was flying in from Minnesota" provides the reader with **bonus information** about Anthony's grandmother and her journey, but it's not essential to the idea that "Anthony went to the airport to pick up his grandmother."

If a nonessential modifier containing bonus information comes **in the middle** of a sentence, it should be separated from the body of the sentence with **two commas:** one before the nonessential modifier, and one after it.

* Mr. Trawley, **who has lived next door for years,** is building a new fence.
    * "Who has lived next door for years" is bonus information about Mr. Trawley. It has commas on both sides of it to show that it's nonessential to the idea that "Mr. Trawley is building a new fence."

* Cinnamon, **which comes from the bark of a particular tree,** is a delicious and valuable spice.
    * "Which comes from the bark of a particular tree" is bonus information about cinnamon. It has commas on both sides of it to show that it's nonessential to the idea that "Cinnamon is a delicious and valuable spice."

From "The Time Machine"

By H.G. Wells

The thing the Time Traveller held in his hand was a glittering metallic framework, scarcely larger than a small clock, and very delicately made. There was ivory in it, and some transparent crystalline substance. And now I must be explicit, for this that follows—unless his explanation is to be accepted—is an absolutely unaccountable thing. He took one of the small octagonal tables that were scattered about the room, and set it in front of the fire, with two legs on the hearthrug. On this table he placed the mechanism. Then he drew up a chair, and sat down. The only other object on the table was a small shaded lamp, the bright light of which fell upon the model. There were also perhaps a dozen candles about, two in brass candlesticks upon the mantel and several in sconces, so that the room was brilliantly illuminated. I sat in a low armchair nearest the fire, and I drew this forward so as to be almost between the Time Traveller and the fireplace. Filby sat behind him, looking over his shoulder. The Medical Man and the Provincial Mayor watched him in profile from the right, the Psychologist from the left. The Very Young Man stood behind the Psychologist. We were all on the alert. It appears incredible to me that any kind of trick, however subtly conceived and however adroitly done, could have been played upon us under these conditions.

The Time Traveller looked at us, and then at the mechanism. "Well?" said the Psychologist.

"This little affair," said the Time Traveller, resting his elbows upon the table and pressing his hands together above the apparatus, "is only a model. It is my plan for a machine to travel through time. You will notice that it looks singularly askew, and that there is an odd twinkling appearance about this bar, as though it was in some way unreal." He pointed to the part with his finger. "Also, here is one little white lever, and here is another."

The Medical Man got up out of his chair and peered into the thing. "It's beautifully made," he said."

"It took two years to make," retorted the Time Traveller. Then, when we had all imitated the action of the Medical Man, he said: "Now I want you clearly to understand that this lever, being pressed over, sends the machine gliding into the future, and this other reverses the motion. This saddle represents the seat of a time traveller. Presently I am going to press the lever, and off the machine will go. It will vanish, pass into future Time, and disappear. Have a good look at the thing. Look at the table too, and satisfy yourselves there is no trickery. I don't want to waste this model, and then be told I'm a quack."

1. What is "the thing" that is mentioned in the first sentence of the passage?

_____

_____

2. Why is the Time Traveller concerned people will think he is "a quack?"

_____

_____

3. What is the purpose of the comma in the sentence, "The only other object on the table was a small shaded lamp, the bright light of which fell upon the model"?

   A. To separate the introduction from the main body of the sentence
   B. To create a compound sentence
   C. To separate nonessential (bonus) information from the body of the sentence
   D. To make a short list of descriptive elements

4. Which of these is the best definition for the word "affair" as it is used in Paragraph 3?

   A. Secret
   B. Lie
   C. Project
   D. Relationship

5. Why do you think the characters in this scene have no names? Why might the author identify them based on their professions?

_____

_____

_____

_____

_____

_____

Using Commas to Identify Nonessential Modifiers

Directions: Each sentence below contains some bonus information that needs to be separated from the body of the sentence. That nonessential modifier might come in the middle of a sentence (which requires two commas) or at the end of the sentence (which means you only need one!).

1. Our class president Jackson Quarry is also the captain of the boys' soccer team.

2. Michael forgot his sister's birthday again this year which was a surprise to absolutely nobody.

3. Francesca has been collecting sneakers since she was in the fourth grade when she got her first pair of Air Jordans.

4. My wife's grandmother who is the best cook I know hosts an incredible holiday party every year.

5. All the players on both teams took a knee as the injured player who was a member of the Oakdale Lions was tended to by a medic.

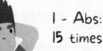

FITNESS

Please be aware of your environment and be safe at all times. If you cannot do an exercise, just try your best.

Repeat these **exercises 4 ROUNDS**

2 - Lunges: 4 times to each leg.
Note: Use your body weight or books as weight to do leg lunges.

4 - Run: 50m
Note: Run 25 meters to one side and 25 meters back to the starting position.

1 - Abs: 15 times

3 - Plank: 20 sec.

From "The Time Machine"

By H.G. Wells

(Continued from Day One's Passage)

There was a minute's pause perhaps. The Psychologist seemed about to speak to me, but changed his mind. Then the Time Traveller put forth his finger towards the lever. "No," he said suddenly. "Lend me your hand." And turning to the Psychologist, he took that individual's hand in his own and told him to put out his forefinger. So that it was the Psychologist himself who sent forth the model Time Machine on its interminable voyage. We all saw the lever turn. I am absolutely certain there was no trickery. There was a breath of wind, and the lamp flame jumped. One of the candles on the mantel was blown out, and the little machine suddenly swung round, became indistinct, was seen as a ghost for a second perhaps, as an eddy of faintly glittering brass and ivory; and it was gone—vanished! Save for the lamp the table was bare.

Everyone was silent for a minute. Then Filby said he was stumped.

The Psychologist recovered from his stupor, and suddenly looked under the table. At that the Time Traveller laughed cheerfully. "Well?" he said, with a reminiscence of the Psychologist. Then, getting up, he went to the tobacco jar on the mantel, and with his back to us began to fill his pipe.

We stared at each other. "Look here," said the Medical Man, "are you in earnest about this? Do you seriously believe that that machine has travelled into time?"

"Certainly," said the Time Traveller, stooping to light a spill at the fire. Then he turned, lighting his pipe, to look at the Psychologist's face. (The Psychologist, to show that he was not unhinged, helped himself to a cigar and tried to light it uncut.) "What is more, I have a big machine nearly finished in there"—he indicated the laboratory—"and when that is put together I mean to have a journey on my own account."

"You mean to say that that machine has travelled into the future?" said Filby.

"Into the future or the past—I don't, for certain, know which."

After an interval the Psychologist had an inspiration. "It must have gone into the past if it has gone anywhere," he said.

"Why?" said the Time Traveller.

"Because I presume that it has not moved in space, and if it travelled into the future it would still be here all this time, since if it travelled into the future it would still be here all this time, since it must have travelled through this time."

1. Why do you think the Time Traveller uses the Psychologist's finger, instead of his own, to push the lever?

_____

_____

2. How is the parenthetical phrase "The Psychologist, to show that he was not unhinged, helped himself to a cigar and tried to light it uncut" an example of irony or humor?

_____

_____

3. Why is the phrase "for certain" comma'd off in the sentence "Into the future or the past—I don't, for certain, know which."

   A. It's being used as a subordinating conjunction to connect the two sentences
   B. It's a nonessential or optional piece of information in the sentence
   C. It's being used as a transition word between ideas
   D. It's the middle item in a list

4. Which of these means the same thing as "Are you in earnest about this?"

   A. Are you stupid?
   B. Have you researched this extensively?
   C. Do you expect me to believe this?
   D. Do you honestly believe this?

5. Explain the Psychologist's logic for why the model must have travelled into the past:

_____

_____

_____

_____

Combining Comma-Placing Skills

Directions: By now, you should know four different ways to use a comma: to make a compound sentence, to separate items in a **list,** to divide an **introduction** from the main body of the sentence, and to identify **nonessential (bonus) information.** It's time to put all those skills together!

The sentences below <u>all</u> need **multiple commas** in order to be correct. Read each sentence carefully and determine where you should place the commas.

1. At the grocery store we picked up apples tomatoes and a jar of pickles.

2. My favorite class is French because Monsieur Francois who is actually from France is an excellent teacher and many other students agree with me.

3. After the earthquake we had to sweep up some shards of shattered glass fragments of decorative plates and dirt from a potted plant which had fallen from a shelf.

4. I burned my hand on a radiator when I was young so I am always extra careful around heaters fireplaces and stoves especially in the winter.

5. That old tree needs to have several branches trimmed or it could create a dangerous situation in the winter when the trees become heavy with snow.

Please be aware of your environment and be safe at all times. If you cannot do an exercise, just try your best.

Repeat these **exercises 4 ROUNDS**

1 - Squats: 15 times. Note: imagine you are trying to sit on a chair.

2 - Side Bending: 10 times to each side. Note: try to touch your feet.

3 - Tree Pose: Stay as long as possible. Note: do the same with the other leg.

Writing algebraic expressions

1. Which of the following expressions best represents: add 4 to X?

   A. X + 4
   B. X − 4
   C. X × 4
   D. X ÷ 4

2. Write an expression for the phrase 'divide 12 by X'.

   A. 12 × X
   B. X × 12
   C. X ÷ 12
   D. 12 ÷ X

3. Which of the following expressions corresponds to A - 6?

   A. Find A less than 6
   B. Subtract 6 from A
   C. Subtract A from 6
   D. Divide 6 by A

4. Determine which of the following expressions best represents: find C times as much as 25.

   A. 25 + C
   B. C ÷ 25
   C. 25 ÷ C
   D. 25 × C

5. Which of the following expressions best represents: give 16 to Y?

   A. 16 × Y   C. Y + 16
   B. 16 - Y   D. Y ÷ 16

6. Which of the following expressions corresponds to M × 8?

   A. Give 8 to M
   B. Multiply M by 8
   C. Find 8 more than M
   D. Give M to 8

7. Determine which of the following expressions best represents: find D times 14.

   A. D − 14
   B. 14 × D
   C. 14 ÷ D
   D. D ÷ 14

8. Which of the following expressions best represents: divide K by 4?

   A. K − 4
   B. 4 × K
   C. K ÷ 4
   D. 4 ÷ K

9. Which of the following expressions corresponds to 65 + X?

   A. Multiply X by 65
   B. Find X times 65
   C. Give X to 65
   D. Subtract 65 from X

10. Which of the following expressions best represents: find 12 more than B?

    A. B + 12   C. 12 × B
    B. B × 12   D. 12 ÷ B

11. Write an expression for the phrase 'subtract M from 26'.

12. Write an expression for the phrase 'find C times 15'.

_____

13. Write an expression for the phrase 'add 8 to D'.

_____

14. Write an expression for the phrase 'multiply Y by 36'.

_____

15. Which expression corresponds to 'give 14 to X'.

A. $X \times 14$ C. $X + 14$

B. $14 \times X$ D. $X - 14$

16. Which expression corresponds to 'K less than 32'.

A. $K - 32$ C. $32 + K$

B. $32 - K$ D. $32 \div K$

17. Which expression is for the operation '9 more than M'?

A. $9 - M$ C. $M + 9$

B. $M \times 9$ D. $M \div 9$

18. Write the phrase 'divide 16 by Y' as as an expression.

_____

19. Write the following phrase as an expression: '5 times as much as X'.

_____

20. Write an expression for the phrase 'subtract F from 28'.

_____

FITNESS

Please be aware of your environment and be safe at all times. If you cannot do an exercise, just try your best.

Repeat these
**exercises
4 ROUNDS**

1 - Bend forward: 15 times.
Note: try to touch your feet. Make sure to keep your back straight and if needed you can bend your knees.

2 - Lunges: 7 times to each leg.
Note: Use your body weight or books as weight to do leg lunges.

3 - Plank: 20 sec.

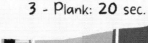

4 - Abs: 15 times

Evaluating expressions

1. Find the value of the expression $25 + x$ if $x = 14$.

_____

2. What is the value of the expression below if $a = 4$?

$$28 \div a + 15$$

A. 18
B. 20
C. 22
D. 25

3. What is the value of the expression below when $x = 5$ and $y = 7$?

$$2 \times x + 4 \times y$$

A. 26 C. 34
B. 30 D. 38

4. What is the value of the expression below if $b = 6$?

$$b^2 - 4b$$

A. 22
B. 12
C. 8
D. 6

5. Find the value of the expression $x \div 4 + 2 \times x$ if $x = 48$.

_____

6. What is the value of the expression below if $k = 16$?

$$54 - k \times (18 - k)$$

A. 22
B. 24
C. 28
D. 30

7. What is the value of the expression below when $a = -3$ and $b = 12$?

$$4a + 2b$$

A. 24
B. -12
C. 12
D. 36

8. Find the area of the triangle, using the formula $A = \frac{1}{2} bh$, where $h = 12$ in and $b = 22$ in.

_____

9. What is the value of the expression $30 - a^2 + 55$, if $a = 9$?

A. -50
B. -4
C. 4
D. 50

10. What is the value of the expression below when $a = \frac{1}{2}$ and $b = 4$?

$$5a \times (6 - b)$$

A. $\frac{1}{2}$

B. $\frac{2}{5}$

C. 5

D. 10

11. Which of the following expressions has the value of $x = 45$?

    A. $x \div 5 + 16 = 24$
    B. $18 - x + 40 = 13$
    C. $(86 - x) \times 4 = 165$
    D. $125 - 2x = 32$

12. Use the formulas $V = s^3$ and $A = 6s^2$ to find the volume and surface area of a cube with a side length of $s = \dfrac{2}{3}$ in.

13. Find the volume of a rectangular prism, using the formula $V = l \times w \times h$, where $h = \dfrac{3}{5}$ cm, $l = 15$ cm, $w = 4$ cm.

14. What is the value of the expression $10x + y \div 4$, if $x = 5$ and $y = 124$?

15. Find the value of the following expressions, if $z = 12$.

    A. $36 - z \div 4$ _____
    B. $-2z + 140$ _____
    C. $25z - \dfrac{1}{2}z^2$ _____
    D. $15z - 28$ _____

16. Use the formulas $V = s^3$ and $A = 6s^2$ to find the volume and surface area of a cube with a side length of $s = 9$ cm.

17. What is the value of the expression $100 - 4a + 28 \div b$, if $a = 45$ and $b = 7$?

18. Find the area of the triangle, using the formula $A = \dfrac{1}{2} bh$, where $h = \dfrac{1}{2}$ in and $b = 1\dfrac{1}{3}$ in.

Please be aware of your environment and be safe at all times. If you cannot do an exercise, just try your best.

Repeat these **exercises** **4 ROUNDS**

1 - High Plank: 20 sec.

2 - Chair: 15 sec.
Note: sit on an imaginary chair, keep your back straight.

4 - Abs: 15 times

3 - Waist Hooping: 15 times. Note: if you do not have a hoop, pretend you have an imaginary hoop and rotate your hips 10 times.

Generating equivalent expressions

1. What is another way to write $12x - 2y + 5$?

   A. $6x - (y + 5)$
   B. $6(x - 2y) + 5$
   C. $2(6x - y) + 5$
   D. $(12 - 2)xy + 5$

2. Which expression can also be written as $5x + 10y - 8y$?

   A. $5(x + y) - 8y$
   B. $5x + 2(5y - 8y)$
   C. $5x + 5 \times 2y$
   D. $5x + y(10 - 8)$

3. Which of the following expressions is the same as $3 - 2x + 4(x - y)$?

   A. $2x + 4y - 3$
   B. $2x - 4y + 3$
   C. $3 - 2(4x - 4y)$
   D. $-8x + 8y = 3$

4. What is another way to write $3x - 2y + 5x + 8y$?

   A. $2(4x + 3y)$
   B. $8y + 6x$
   C. $4(2x + 2y)$
   D. $5x^2 + 6y^2$

5. Which of the following expressions is NOT the same as $2 - x(4 + x) - 2y$?

   A. $2 - 4x - x^2 - 2y$
   B. $2(1 - y) - (x^2 + 4x)$
   C. $2 - 4x(1 - x)$
   D. $2(1 - y) - x(2 + x) - 2x$

6. Which of the following expressions is equivalent to $7(y + 2) - 5x^2$?

   A. $5(1 - x^2) + 7y + 2$
   B. $19 - 5(1 + x^2) + 7y$
   C. $5x(1 + x) + 7y + 2$
   D. $7y + 14 - 5(1 + x)$

7. Choose another way to write $26 - x + 2y - 14$.

   A. $12 - 2(7 - y) - x$
   B. $2(y + 6) - x$
   C. $(6 - y) + x + (6 - y)$
   D. $2(13 - y) - (x - 14)$

8. Which of the following expressions is NOT equivalent to the other three?

   A. $16x - 24y + 8$
   B. $-8(3y - 2x) + 8$
   C. $8(2x - 3y + 1) + 7$
   D. $4(2 - 6y + 4x)$

9. Choose an expression which is equivalent to $12x + 6y - 18$.

   A. $3(4x + 2y) - 6$
   B. $2(6x + 3y) - 9$
   C. $12x - 2(3y + 9)$
   D. $3(4x + 2y - 6)$

10. Which of the following expressions is NOT equivalent to the other three?

   A. $x(2 + x) - 4y + 6$
   B. $6 + 2x - 4y + x^2$
   C. $2(1 - 2y) + x + x^2 + 6$
   D. $2(3 - 2y) + x^2 + 2x$

11. Write an equivalent expression for $x + y \times y + x$.

12. What is another way to write $6(3x + 10y)$?

13. What is another way to write $42x + 18y$?

14. Write an equivalent expression for $2x(1 - 3x)$, applying the distributive property.

15. Simplify the expression: $6(1 + x) + 5(2y - 4)$.

16. Write an equivalent expression for $3x + 6y - 2x + 4y$, by simplifying the given expression.

17. What is another way to write $(x - 1)y + 7$?

18. What is another way to write $3(2x^2 - x)$?

19. Simplify the expression: $6(3 + 12x) - (2y + 18)$.

20. Write an equivalent expression for $5x(5x + 4)$, applying the distributive property.

YOGA

Please be aware of your environment and be safe at all times. If you cannot do an exercise, just try your best.

1 - Down Dog: 25 sec.

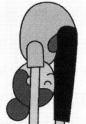

2 - Bend Down: 25 sec.

3 - Chair: 20 sec.

4 - Child Pose: 25 sec.

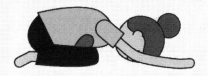

5 - Shavasana: as long as you can. Note: think of happy moments and relax your mind.

Digestion

Over the last few weeks, we've taken some time to think about some of our major organs. We've talked about the way the heart and lungs provide oxygen to the rest of the body, but it's time to talk about another crucial organ: the **stomach**. Your stomach has the important role of preparing your food to be turned into fuel by your body. After we break up our food with our teeth and saliva, it goes into our stomach where strong **acid** breaks that food down into an easier-to-process form.

Today, we'll make a quick, easy model of a stomach and observe what it looks like when food is in the early stages of being digested.

Materials:

* 1 large plastic freezer bag with zipper top
* 1 packet of saltine crackers
* About a cup of lemon juice
* Notepaper
* A stopwatch or timer

Procedure:

1. Before beginning your experiment, double-check your freezer bag and ensure that its zipper top works properly and that there are no leaks or holes. This bag is going to represent a stomach, so we need it to be able to hold fluid.

2. Pour the lemon juice into the bottom of the bag to add acid to the stomach.

3. Crush up a few crackers in your hand (or you can put them in another zipper bag and hit them a few times with a can or kitchen tool), smashing them into pieces to simulate the way your teeth break down your food before it heads to your stomach.

4. On your notepaper, make a prediction about what will happen when you add the crackers to the acid.

5. Drop the crushed up crackers into the bag of lemon juice and **start your timer**. Seal the bag tightly, and be sure to let out any excess air that's above the juice before you close the zipper.

6. Once your bag is sealed, hold it up and examine what the crackers look like in the acid, and write down a brief description in your notes.

7. Give the bag a slight shake to simulate the churning of your stomach. You can even give the bag a little squeeze to reflect the role your abdominal muscles play in stimulating digestion.

8. After three minutes, look at the crackers through the bag again and make note how they have changed.

9. After another five minutes, check the crackers again and describe them in your notes.

10. After fifteen more minutes, carefully drain the bag (making sure not to get any mushy crackers in the sink) and see what the crackers look like after a little less than a half hour in the "stomach". Write a description in your notes and compare it to the prediction you made back in Step 4.

Follow-Up Questions:

1. Based on what you saw today, how do you think it would affect your stomach if you ate something that made it **less** acidic?

_____

_____

_____

2. Based on what you saw today, how do you think it would affect your stomach if you ate something that made it **more** acidic?

_____

_____

_____

YOGA

Please be aware of your environment and be safe at all times. If you cannot do an exercise, just try your best.

1 - Tree Pose: Stay as long as possible. Note: do on one leg then on another.

4 - Lower Plank: 12 sec. Note: Keep your back straight and body tight.

2 - Down Dog: 25 sec.

5 - Book Pose: 15 sec. Note: Keep your core tight. Legs should be across from your eyes.

3 - Stretching: Stay as long as possible. Note: do on one leg then on another.

6 - Shavasana: 5 min. Note: this pose is very important and provides you with long term benefits. Try not to skip this. Close your eyes and imagine who you want to be and what your goals are! Always think happy thoughts.

Task: Help Santa deliver presents, through the chimneys (don't miss any!). Use stairs and ladders. For Santa's safety, don't climb or jump up the walls.

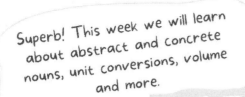

Superb! This week we will learn about abstract and concrete nouns, unit conversions, volume and more.

WEEK 8

Some species of dinosaurs such as the Dromiceiomimus ran extremely fast (about 37 miles per hour)!

Abstract vs. Concrete

We use nouns to represent all sorts of people, places, things and ideas in the English language. However, as you've probably noticed, some nouns represent things or ideas that don't really have a physical form. We refer to those concepts as **abstract nouns.** On the other hand, if a noun is something that you can see or experience in a real, physical way, we call those **concrete nouns.**

It's important to understand the distinction between abstract and concrete nouns to ensure that your writing is as clear and descriptive as possible. If you only use abstract words, readers may find your writing hard to follow. On the other hand, if you only use concrete concepts, readers might find your writing shallow and boring.

Key Terms

Noun: A person, place, thing, or idea

Concrete Noun: A person, place, thing, or idea that can be experienced using one of the five senses (touch, taste, smell, hearing, or sight).

Abstract Noun: A thing, concept, or idea that cannot be experienced using one of the five senses.

For Example...

* Mark and Linda are best friends.

    * Mark & Linda are both **concrete nouns** because they are people. If you knew Mark or Linda, you could describe what they look like, explain their personality, etc.

    * "Friends" is also a concrete noun because, if you have a friend, you can describe them in depth. They are a real, concrete object in your life.

* Mark and Linda have a terrific friendship.

    * Mark and Linda are still **concrete** because they're people

    * Friendship, however, is an **abstract noun** because it is a concept or idea. You can't go to the store and buy a pound of friendship, and you can't "see" friendship, even though you can see the things you do with your friends.

* Albert Einstein believed that imagination was more important than intelligence.

    * Albert Einstein is a **concrete noun** because he was a real person. Pictures exist showing what he looked like, and people who knew him can describe his personality.

    * Imagination and intelligence are both **abstract nouns** because they represent **concepts that you can't see or experience with your senses.** They're **ideas,** not objects or people that you can interact with.

From "Treasure Island"

By Robert Louis Stevenson

Aboard ship he carried his crutch by a lanyard round his neck, to have both hands as free as possible. It was something to see him wedge the foot of the crutch against a bulkhead, and propped against it, yielding to every movement of the ship, get on with his cooking like someone safe ashore. Still more strange was it to see him in the heaviest of weather cross the deck. He had a line or two rigged up to help him across the widest spaces—Long John's earrings, they were called; and he would hand himself from one place to another, now using the crutch, now trailing it alongside by the lanyard, as quickly as another man could walk. Yet some of the men who had sailed with him before expressed their pity to see him so reduced.

"He's no common man, Barbecue," said the coxswain to me. "He had good schooling in his young days and can speak like a book when so minded; and brave—a lion's nothing alongside of Long John! I seen him grapple four and knock their heads together—him unarmed."

All the crew respected and even obeyed him. He had a way of talking to each and doing everybody some particular service. To me he was unweariedly kind, and always glad to see me in the galley, which he kept as clean as a new pin, the dishes hanging up burnished and his parrot in a cage in one corner.

"Come away, Hawkins," he would say; "come and have a yarn with John. Nobody more welcome than yourself, my son. Sit you down and hear the news. Here's Cap'n Flint—I calls my parrot Cap'n Flint, after the famous buccaneer—here's Cap'n Flint predicting success to our v'yage. Wasn't you, cap'n?"

And the parrot would say, with great rapidity, "Pieces of eight! Pieces of eight! Pieces of eight!" till you wondered that it was not out of breath, or till John threw his handkerchief over the cage.

1. How do Long John's personality and reputation contrast with his physical appearance?

    _____

    _____

2. Based on the passage, describe the relationship that Long John and Jim Hawkins seem to have in your own words.

    _____

    _____

3. Based on the passage, which of these statements is definitely true about Long John?

    A. He is missing a leg
    B. He has a peg leg
    C. He has some form of disability that impacts his walking
    D. He always has to use crutches

4. Why does John sometimes throw his handkerchief over the parrot's cage?

    A. To make it stop squawking
    B. To make it take a nap
    C. To prevent it from overhearing secret conversations
    D. To keep the parrot from scaring Jim Hawkins

5. Based on what you read in the passage, make a **prediction** about what might happen to Long John and Jim Hawkins later in the book. What does this scene seem to be suggesting or foreshadowing might happen?

    _____

    _____

    _____

    _____

    _____

Abstract or Concrete?

Directions: Read each sentence below. Then, think about the <u>underlined</u> words and determine whether they represent **concrete** people, places, or things or **abstract** concepts or ideas. Write your answers on the lines below each sentence.

1.   The quick brown <u>fox</u> jumped over the lazy <u>dog</u>.

Fox: _____

Dog: _____

2.   <u>Spaghetti</u> and <u>meatballs</u> for dinner sounds like a great <u>plan</u>.

Spaghetti: _____

Meatballs: _____

Plan: _____

3.   Our history <u>textbook</u> gave me a great <u>understanding</u> of the Aztec <u>culture</u>.

Textbook: _____

Understanding: _____

Culture: _____

4.   The <u>object</u> of <u>bowling</u> is to knock down all the <u>pins</u> using a heavy <u>ball</u>.

Object: _____

Bowling: _____

Pins: _____

Ball: _____

FITNESS

Please be aware of your environment and be safe at all times. If you cannot do an exercise, just try your best.

Repeat these **exercises** 4 ROUNDS

1 - Abs: 15 times

2 - Lunges: 4 times to each leg.
Note: Use your body weight or books as weight to do leg lunges.

3 - Plank: 20 sec.

"Treasure Island"

By Robert Louis Stevenson

(Continued from Day One's Passage)

We had some heavy weather, which only proved the qualities of the Hispaniola. Every man on board seemed well content, and they must have been hard to please if they had been otherwise, for it is my belief there was never a ship's company so spoiled since Noah put to sea. Double grog was going on the least excuse; there was duff on odd days, as, for instance, if the squire heard it was any man's birthday, and always a barrel of apples standing broached in the waist for anyone to help himself that had a fancy.

"Never knew good come of it yet," the captain said to Dr. Livesey. "Spoil forecastle hands, make devils. That's my belief."

But good did come of the apple barrel, as you shall hear, for if it had not been for that, we should have had no note of warning and might all have perished by the hand of treachery.

This was how it came about.

We had run up the trades to get the wind of the island we were after—I am not allowed to be more plain—and now we were running down for it with a bright lookout day and night. It was about the last day of our outward voyage by the largest computation; some time that night, or at latest before noon of the morrow, we should sight the Treasure Island. We were heading S.S.W. and had a steady breeze abeam and a quiet sea. The Hispaniola rolled steadily, dipping her bowsprit now and then with a whiff of spray. All was drawing alow and aloft; everyone was in the bravest spirits because we were now so near an end of the first part of our adventure.

Now, just after sundown, when all my work was over and I was on my way to my berth, it occurred to me that I should like an apple. I ran on deck. The watch was all forward looking out for the island. The man at the helm was watching the luff of the sail and whistling away gently to himself, and that was the only sound excepting the swish of the sea against the bows and around the sides of the ship.

In I got bodily into the apple barrel, and found there was scarce an apple left; but sitting down there in the dark, what with the sound of the waters and the rocking movement of the ship, I had either fallen asleep or was on the point of doing so when a heavy man sat down with rather a clash close by. The barrel shook as he leaned his shoulders against it, and I was just about to jump up when the man began to speak. It was Silver's voice, and before I had heard a dozen words, I would not have shown myself for all the world, but lay there, trembling and listening, in the extreme of fear and curiosity, for from these dozen words I understood that the lives of all the honest men aboard depended upon me alone.

1. Why does the narrator (Jim Hawkins) believe the crew of the Hispaniola is "spoiled?"

_____

_____

2. How does Jim Hawkins get stuck in the apple barrel?

_____

_____

3. What does Jim's statement "I am not allowed to be more plain" suggest about the island?

   A. Jim doesn't fully understand the location of the island
   B. Jim doesn't know the name of the island
   C. The specific name and location of the island are still guarded secrets
   D. Jim is concerned the island is mythical and doesn't really exist

4. Which of these statements from the text is an example of **foreshadowing?**

   A. "We had some heavy weather, which only proved the qualities of the Hispaniola..."
   B. "But good did come of the apple barrel, as you shall hear..."
   C. "The Hispaniola rolled steadily and aloft; everyone was in the bravest spirits..."
   D. "The watch was all forward look out for the island..."

5. Based on the tone of the final paragraph, we know Jim hears something really important while he is stuck in the apple barrel. Based on this passage (and Day One's passage as well, if you like), what kind of conversation do you predict Jim hears?

_____

_____

_____

_____

Finding & Identifying Abstract & Concrete Nouns

Directions: Each sentence below contains **three** different nouns (people, places, things, ideas). First, read the sentence and <u>underline</u> the three nouns. Then, on the lines below, write whether each one is abstract or concrete.

1. There is a popular myth that George Washington got caught cutting down a tree.

   _____   _____   _____

2. To be a writer, you must have a great imagination and a lot of confidence

   _____   _____   _____

3. The pitcher displayed extreme focus as he watched the baserunner.

   _____   _____   _____

4. The food on airplanes is often of very low quality.

   _____   _____   _____

5. The happy puppy ran across the floor, filled with enthusiasm.

   _____   _____   _____

FITNESS

Please be aware of your environment and be safe at all times. If you cannot do an exercise, just try your best.

Repeat these **exercises 4 ROUNDS**

2 - Side Bending: 10 times to each side. Note: try to touch your feet.

3 - Tree Pose: Stay as long as possible. Note: do the same with the other leg.

1 - Squats: 15 times. Note: imagine you are trying to sit on a chair.

Converting measurements

1. A dog weighed 15 pounds and 6 ounces. What is the weight of 4 such dogs in ounces?

   A. 944 ounces
   B. 954 ounces
   C. 984 ounces
   D. 994 ounces

2. A runner ran for 96 yards. How many feet did he run?

   A. 260 feet
   B. 266 feet
   C. 280 feet
   D. 288 feet

3. A bag of flour is 20 pounds 9 ounces. How much does the bag of flour weigh in ounces?

   A. 318 ounces
   B. 320 ounces
   C. 329 ounces
   D. 330 ounces

4. Peter is 152 centimeters tall. How tall is Peter in meters?

   A. 0.0152 meters
   B. 0.152 meters
   C. 1.52 meters
   D. 15.2 meters

5. The tool box is 7 kilograms and 150 grams. What is the weight of the box in grams?

   A. 7.15 grams
   B. 71.5 grams
   C. 715 grams
   D. 7,150 grams

6. A bridge has a length of 98 yards. How long is the bridge in feet?

   A. 290 feet
   B. 294 feet
   C. 296 feet
   D. 298 feet

7. A barrel of water is 120 gallons. How many pints of water is in the barrel?

   A. 960 pints
   B. 980 pints
   C. 989 pints
   D. 990 pints

8. Logan needs 20 meters of rope. Each rope is 500 centimeters. How many ropes does Logan need?

   A. 2
   B. 3
   C. 4
   D. 4.5

9. The length of a table is 4 feet and 4 inches. What is the length of the table in inches?

   A. 48 inches
   B. 52 inches
   C. 56 inches
   D. 60 inches

10. If a package of sugar weighs 1.45 kilograms, how many grams does the package of sugar weigh?

    A. 145 grams

    B. 1,450 grams

    C. 14,500 grams

    D. 145,000 grams

11. Emma bought 5 pints of milk. How much milk did she buy in quarts?

    A. $\dfrac{1}{2}$

    B. $1\dfrac{1}{2}$

    C. $2\dfrac{1}{2}$

    D. $2\dfrac{1}{4}$

12. Mia has five packages of nuts. Each package weighs $\dfrac{1}{4}$ of a pound. How many ounces of nuts does Mia have?

13. Christopher ran 0.8 kilometers on Friday and 0.75 kilometers on Saturday. How many meters did he run in total?

14. The table is 820 millimeters tall. How tall is the table in meters?

    A. 82 meters

    B. 8.2 meters

    C. 0.82 meters

    D. 0.082 meters

15. A company is installing an electrical cable that will be 4 km long. There is already 750 meters of electrical cable on one side and 22,800 cm of electrical cable from the other side. How many kilometers of electrical cable still has to be installed?

16. Gabriel started training at 6:15 pm. He spent 95 minutes training. What time did he finish his training?

17. The lake is 125 meters wide. How many millimeters wide is the lake?

18. A box of candy weighs 344 ounces. How much does the box weigh in pounds?

FITNESS

Please be aware of your environment and be safe at all times. If you cannot do an exercise, just try your best.

Repeat these **exercises 4 ROUNDS**

2 - Lunges: 7 times to each leg.
Note: Use your body weight or books as weight to do leg lunges.

1 - Bend forward: 15 times.
Note: try to touch your feet. Make sure to keep your back straight and if needed you can bend your knees.

3 - Plank: 20 sec.

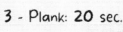

4 - Abs: 15 times

Line plot to display data

Several students recorded their jump distance. Their distances are shown below. Use the information to answer questions 1 - 3.

Distance jumped (in yards)

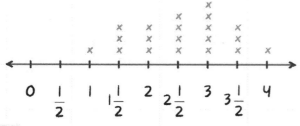

1. What was the distance most students jumped?

   A. $1\frac{1}{2}$ yards   C. 3 yards

   B. $2\frac{1}{2}$ yards   D. $3\frac{1}{2}$ yards

2. What was the combined distance jumped by the students?

   A. 36 yards   C. $48\frac{1}{2}$ yards

   B. $40\frac{1}{2}$ yards   D. 51 yards

3. If the total distance remained the same but each student jumped the same distance, how many meters would each student jump?

   A. $2\frac{10}{15}$ meters

   B. $2\frac{11}{20}$ meters

   C. $2\frac{6}{10}$ meters

   D. $2\frac{12}{14}$ meters

Below is some data about the amount of milk some fifth grade students drank. Use the data set to answer questions 4 - 6.

Milk (in gallons)

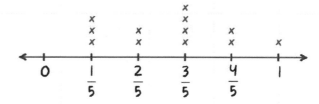

4. How much milk did the students drink on in total according to the data above?

   A. $5\frac{4}{5}$ gallons

   B. $6\frac{2}{5}$ gallons

   C. $6\frac{3}{5}$ gallons

   D. 7 gallons

5. If all the milk had been equally distributed to the students, how much milk would each student receive?

   A. $\frac{4}{15}$ gallons   C. $\frac{8}{15}$ gallons

   B. $\frac{6}{15}$ gallons   D. $\frac{9}{15}$ gallons

6. If the sixth grade class drank $1\frac{1}{2}$ times the amount of milk as the fifth grade class, how many glasses of milk would the sixth grade students drink?

   A. 9 gallons

   B. $9\frac{1}{5}$ gallons

   C. $9\frac{2}{5}$ gallons

143

D. $9\frac{3}{5}$ gallons

C. $1\frac{5}{16}$ pounds   D. $1\frac{2}{9}$ pounds

Mr. Bergen's class collected food for the local food bank. The contributions are shown below. Use the information to answer questions 7 - 9

The line plot below shows the volume (in liters) of syrup in bottles. Use the given data to answer questions 10 - 12.

Food Donated (pounds)

Syrup bottles (in liters)

7. How many pounds of food did Mr. Bergen's class donate?

   A. $15\frac{3}{4}$ pounds   C. $16\frac{3}{4}$ pounds

   B. $16\frac{1}{4}$ pounds   D. $17\frac{2}{4}$ pounds

8. How many students donated to the food bank?

   A. 10   C. 16

   B. 14   D. 20

9. If the amount collected by them was the same and everyone gave the same amount, how many pounds would each student give?

   A. $1\frac{4}{20}$ pounds   B. $1\frac{3}{32}$ pounds

10. What is the total amount of all syrup?

    A. $5\frac{2}{3}$ liters   C. 7 liters

    B. $6\frac{1}{3}$ liters   D. $9\frac{1}{3}$ liters

11. If you were to redistribute the syrup, so each bottle had the same amount, what volume would each bottle have?

    A. $\frac{3}{4}$ liters   C. $\frac{12}{28}$ liters

    B. $\frac{14}{15}$ liters   D. $\frac{8}{12}$ liters

12. How many bottles are there?

RoARRr

Please be aware of your environment and be safe at all times. If you cannot do an exercise, just try your best.

FITNESS

Repeat these exercises 4 ROUNDS

1 - High Plank: 20 sec.

2 - Chair: 15 sec.
Note: sit on an imaginary chair, keep your back straight.

3 - Waist Hooping: 15 times.
Note: if you do not have a hoop, pretend you have an imaginary hoop and rotate your hips 10 times.

4 - Abs: 15 times

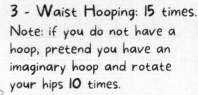

Volume

1. Find the volume of the shape.

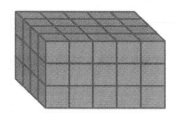

A. 54 cubic units
B. 56 cubic units
C. 60 cubic units
D. 62 cubic units

2. Find the volume of the figure below.

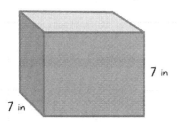

7 in
7 in
12 in

A. 544 cubic inches
B. 588 cubic inches
C. 612 cubic inches
D. 628 cubic inches

3. Find the volume of the shape.

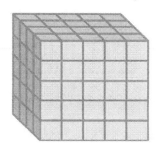

A. 75 cubic units
B. 78 cubic units
C. 96 cubic units
D. 100 cubic units

4. Find the volume of the rectangular prism.

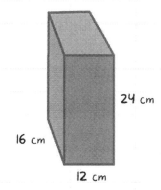

24 cm
16 cm
12 cm

A. 4,388 cubic centimeters
B. 4,468 cubic centimeters
C. 4,608 cubic centimeters
D. 4,988 cubic centimeters

5. Find the volume of the cube.

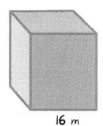

16 m

A. 4,096 cubic meters
B. 4,356 cubic meters
C. 4,686 cubic meters
D. 5,086 cubic meters

6. What is the volume of this object?

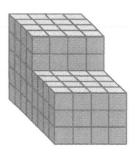

A. 84 cubic units
B. 88 cubic units
C. 128 cubic units
D. 98 cubic units

7. Find the volume of this object.

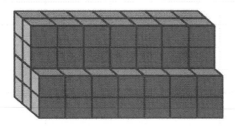

A. 64 cubic units
B. 70 cubic units
C. 49 cubic units
D. 46 cubic units

9. What is the volume of this object?

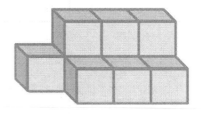

A. 6 cubic units
B. 8 cubic units
C. 10 cubic units
D. 12 cubic units

8. Find the volume of the figure below.

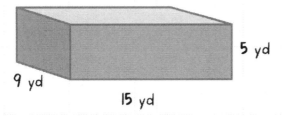

5 yd

9 yd

15 yd

A. 545 cubic yards
B. 615 cubic yards
C. 625 cubic yards
D. 675 cubic yards

10. Find the volume of the rectangular prism.

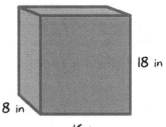

18 in

8 in

16 in

A. 2,304 cubic inches
B. 2,434 cubic inches
C. 2,564 cubic inches
D. 2,644 cubic inches

YOGA

Please be aware of your environment and be safe at all times. If you cannot do an exercise, just try your best.

1 - Down Dog: 25 sec.

2 - Bend Down: 25 sec.

3 - Chair: 20 sec.

5 - Shavasana: as long as you can. Note: think of happy moments and relax your mind.

Creating a Food Web

Last week, we looked at how a stomach digests food. Next, we'll tackle the question of where exactly that food comes from for many of the animals on our planet. When we discuss an **ecosystem** or area with a specific climate, features, group of plants, and collection of animals, it's always important to think about the **food chain or food web**. A food web is a visual organizer that helps people understand where different animals in a given place or environment get their food.

Today, we'll be doing a little research, a little art, and learning a lot about interactions between different animals and plants across the food web.

Materials:

* At least 12 blank index cards
* Art supplies (colored pencils, markers, crayons, etc.)
* An encyclopedia or internet access for research
* Notepaper
* A camera (or cell phone)

Procedure:

1. Begin by taking 4 index cards and writing each of the following names at the top of one of the cards: **Grass, Wild Raspberries, Wildflowers, Mayfly**

2. Using your encyclopedia or the internet, research each of those four organisms. Directly under the title you wrote on each card in Step 1, draw a picture of the organism. On the other side of the index card, write down **at least five** important facts about that organism. Make sure to think about its role in the food chain!

3. Take 4 more index cards and write each of the following names of the top of one of the cards: **Mouse, Grasshopper, Pine Warbler, Bass**

4. Using your encyclopedia or the internet, research each of those four organisms. Directly under the title you wrote on each card in Step 3, draw a picture of the organism. On the other side of the index card, write down **at least five** important facts about that organism. Make sure to think about its role in the food chain!

5. Take your final 4 index cards and write each of the following names of the top of one of the cards: **Deer, Bobcat, Red-tailed Hawk, Mink**

6. Using your encyclopedia or the internet, research each of those four organisms. Directly under the title you wrote on each card in Step 5, draw a picture of the organism. On the other side of the index card, write down **at least five** important facts about that organism. Make sure to think about its role in the food chain!

7. After you've completed all 12 cards, spread them out on a tabletop or the floor and start to think about how those organisms would be interacting in an ecosystem. Which ones are primarily predators? Which ones are primarily prey? Which ones would be scared of which other ones?

8. After you've taken some time to think, move your cards around and arrange them into a web, tree, or chain in a way that reflects their relationships in nature. Once your layout is complete, take a picture of it so that you can refer to it whenever you want.

Follow-Up Questions:

1. Provide an example of how one of the 12 organisms you researched plays a crucial role in the food chain/web.

_____

_____

_____

2. Based on what you saw as you explored, how are smaller, less important organisms that we don't think about much just as important as the big, impressive ones?

_____

_____

_____

 YOGA

Please be aware of your environment and be safe at all times. If you cannot do an exercise, just try your best.

1 - Tree Pose: Stay as long as possible. Note: do on one leg then on another.

2 - Down Dog: 25 sec.

3 - Stretching: Stay as long as possible. Note: do on one leg then on another.

4 - Lower Plank: 12 sec. Note: Keep your back straight and body tight.

5 - Book Pose: 15 sec. Note: Keep your core tight. Legs should be across from your eyes.

6 - Shavasana: 5 min. Note: this pose is very important and provides you with long term benefits. Try not to skip this. Close your eyes and imagine who you want to be and what your goals are! Always think happy thoughts.

Task: Time for a crossword puzzle! There are twelve images below. Complete the crossword puzzle by writing the name for each of the images shown.

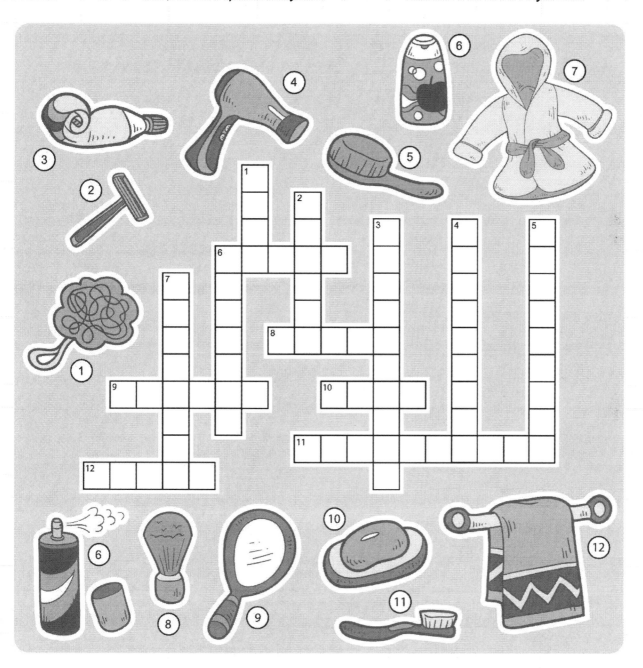

Outstanding job! In week 9 we will learn about quotation marks, line of symmetry, coordinate plane and more.

WEEK 9

The Mesozoic Era is the time period when dinosaurs lived on planet Earth. During this era, the temperature of the planet was different compared to today. The climate was warmer and sea levels were higher.

Quotation Marks & Dialogue

Most great stories contain **dialogue**, or conversations between the characters, that drive the story and reveal important details about characters' personalities. However, formatting dialogue has a few specific rules. **Quotation marks** must be used so that the reader can quickly identify what is being said. On the other hand, commas are used to separate and create transitions between **what the characters are saying** and **who is saying it.**

On the other hand, as you begin to write more complex research essays, you may need to provide quoted material from other texts or scholars. In those situations, it's important to be able to know how to use quotation marks as well!

Key Terms

Quotation Marks: Symbols used to indicate when a character is talking or certain material is quoted from somewhere else (They look "like this!").

Hint:

In order to punctuate dialogue or quotations properly, you need to be able to determine **who** is speaking or being quoted and **what they are saying.** Once you've identified those elements, it's just a matter of inserting punctuation!

For Example...

❊ Trevor said, "I want to be the quarterback."

* "**I want to be the quarterback**" is in quotation marks to show that it is what Trevor said.
  * Notice how the period is **inside** the quotation marks.
* The **comma** goes between the part of the sentence that explains who is talking and the part of the sentence that shows what they are saying.

OR

❊ "I want to be the quarterback," Trevor said.

* "**I want to be the quarterback**" is in quotation marks to show that it is what Trevor said.
  * Notice how the **comma** is **inside** the quotation marks to separate the quoted material from the section of the sentence that explains who said it.

If you have a longer sentence, you can even put the attribution (the part that says who was talking) in the middle!

❊ "Am I crazy," Dante asked, "or do you guys smell bananas?"

* "Am I crazy, or do you guys smell bananas?" is what Dante is saying. Therefore, all those words go in quotation marks.
* **Commas** are used to indicate when the author is transitioning in and out of quoted materials.
* Notice that the **question mark** at the end of the sentence is **inside the quotation marks** to show that it was Dante (not the narrator) who is asking a question.

From "The Call of the Wild"

By Jack London

Buck did not read the newspapers, or he would have known that trouble was brewing, not alone for himself, but for every tide-water dog, strong of muscle and with warm, long hair, from Puget Sound to San Diego. Because men, groping in the Arctic darkness, had found a yellow metal, and because steamship and transportation companies were booming the find, thousands of men were rushing into the Northland. These men wanted dogs, and the dogs they wanted were heavy dogs, with strong muscles by which to toil, and furry coats to protect them from the frost.

Buck lived at a big house in the sun-kissed Santa Clara Valley. Judge Miller's place, it was called. It stood back from the road, half hidden among the trees, through which glimpses could be caught of the wide cool veranda that ran around its four sides. The house was approached by gravelled driveways which wound about through wide-spreading lawns and under the interlacing boughs of tall poplars. At the rear things were on even a more spacious scale than at the front. There were great stables, where a dozen grooms and boys held forth, rows of vine-clad servants' cottages, an endless and orderly array of outhouses, long grape arbors, green pastures, orchards, and berry patches. Then there was the pumping plant for the artesian well, and the big cement tank where Judge Miller's boys took their morning plunge and kept cool in the hot afternoon.

And over this great demesne Buck ruled. Here he was born, and here he had lived the four years of his life. It was true, there were other dogs, There could not but be other dogs on so vast a place, but they did not count. They came and went, resided in the populous kennels, or lived obscurely in the recesses of the house after the fashion of Toots, the Japanese pug, or Ysabel, the Mexican hairless,—strange creatures that rarely put nose out of doors or set foot to ground. On the other hand, there were the fox terriers, a score of them at least, who yelped fearful promises at Toots and Ysabel looking out of the windows at them and protected by a legion of housemaids armed with brooms and mops.

VELOCIRAPTOR

1. Using your own words, describe the area where Buck lives:

_____

_____

2. How is Buck different from the other dogs who live in his area?

_____

_____

3. According to the passage, why is trouble brewing for all the big dogs on the west coast?

   A. Big dogs are going out of style in the area
   B. People are trying to make dogs illegal
   C. People are attacking dogs with brooms and mops
   D. People are looking for dogs to do work in the Northland

4. Which of these is the best definition for "demesne" as it is used in Paragraph 3?

   A. Problem
   B. Situation
   C. Property
   D. Adventure

5. How does the author **personify** Buck? What human traits or characteristics does he seem to have?

_____

_____

_____

_____

_____

_____

Punctuating Dialogue and Quotations

Directions: Each sentence below contains some kind of a quotation or a piece of a conversation but lacks proper punctuation! Using your pen, **add commas and quotation marks as necessary** to make everything as clear as possible for the reader.

1. Clean your room! my mom shouted from downstairs.

2. Mr. Shapiro rolled his eyes and said I guess we're going to need to buy new towels.

3. I am not a good dancer at all Michelle said with a frown and I don't want to embarrass myself.

4. According to Einstein, Anyone who has never made a mistake has never tried anything new.

5. What's all that racket down there? Mrs. Trowley called from upstairs. I'm trying to get some sleep!

Please be aware of your environment and be safe at all times. If you cannot do an exercise, just try your best.

Repeat these **exercises 4 ROUNDS**

2 - Lunges: 4 times to each leg.
Note: Use your body weight or books as weight to do leg lunges.

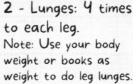

4 - Run: 50m
Note: Run 25 meters to one side and 25 meters back to the starting position.

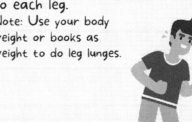

1 - Abs: 15 times

3 - Plank: 20 sec.

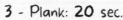

From "The Call of the Wild"

By Jack London

(Continued from Day One's Passage)

And this was the manner of dog Buck was in the fall of 1897, when the Klondike strike dragged men from all the world into the frozen North. But Buck did not read the newspapers, and he did not know that Manuel, one of the gardener's helpers, was an undesirable acquaintance. Manuel had one besetting sin. He loved to play Chinese lottery. Also, in his gambling, he had one besetting weakness—faith in a system; and this made his damnation certain. For to play a system requires money, while the wages of a gardener's helper do not lap over the needs of a wife and numerous progeny.

The Judge was at a meeting of the Raisin Growers' Association, and the boys were busy organizing an athletic club, on the memorable night of Manuel's treachery. No one saw him and Buck go off through the orchard on what Buck imagined was merely a stroll. And with the exception of a solitary man, no one saw them arrive at the little flag station known as College Park. This man talked with Manuel, and money clinked between them.

"You might wrap up the goods before you deliver him," the stranger said gruffly, and Manuel doubled a piece of stout rope around Buck's neck under the collar.

"Twist it, and you'll choke him," said Manuel, and the stranger grunted a ready affirmative.

uck had accepted the rope with quiet dignity. To be sure, it was an unwonted performance: but he had learned to trust in men he knew, and to give them credit for a wisdom that outreached his own. But when the ends of the rope were placed in the stranger's hands, he growled menacingly. He had merely intimated his displeasure, in his pride believing that to intimate was to command.

1.   What things make Manuel "an undesirable acquaintance?"

     _____

     _____

2.   In your own words, what does Manuel do to Buck in this scene?

     _____

     _____

3.   How would describe the **tone** of the conversation between Manuel and the stranger?

     A.   Threatening
     B.   Uplifting
     C.   Sarcastic
     D.   Casual

4.   Why does Buck Growl at the end of the passage?

     A.   He is angry at Manuel for betraying him
     B.   He does not like the rope being put around his neck
     C.   He sees another dog
     D.   He does not like the idea of being handed over to a stranger

5.   Based on the text, what do you predict is going to happen to Buck next?

     _____

     _____

     _____

     _____

     _____

     _____

Punctuating Dialogue

Directions: The block of text represents a conversation between two characters: **Teddy** and **Yosana**. However, reading this dialogue is pretty confusing because it's lacking a lot of the proper punctuation and formatting. Using your pen, write in commas and quotation marks as needed to clarify what is going on and make the dialogue easier to follow.

Teddy and Yosana walked out of the school building and looked up at the bright, blue sky.

It's a beautiful day Yosana marveled.

Definitely Teddy agreed it's so nice to be out of class for the day.

I know! I almost hate to go home too fast she agreed.

Do you want to hang out at the park over by the library for a while? Teddy suggested. I have a flying disc in my backpack.

Yosana replied That sounds like fun, but I need to call my mom first to tell her where I m going.

That's a good idea Teddy agreed. I will text my parents as well.

Teddy and Yosana walked to the park, where they threw the flying disc back and forth for about an hour. Eventually, Yosana looked at her phone and noticed it was getting late.

I have to be home by five she explained because I have to make sure the dog goes for a walk before my parents get home.

That's fine Teddy said with a smile. Let me walk you home.

Yosana smiled and said Thank you very much!

FITNESS

Please be aware of your environment and be safe at all times. If you cannot do an exercise, just try your best.

Repeat these **exercises 4 ROUNDS**

2 - Side Bending: 10 times to each side. Note: try to touch your feet.

3 - Tree Pose: Stay as long as possible. Note: do the same with the other leg.

1 - Squats: 15 times. Note: imagine you are trying to sit on a chair.

Line of symmetry

1. Is the shape below symmetrical?

_____

2. How many lines of symmetry does this shape have?

A. 0
B. 1
C. 3
D. 5

3. In which shape is the line passing through the shape a line of symmetry?

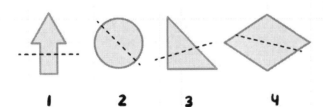

A. 1
B. 2
C. 3
D. 4

4. In the shape below, which of the lines shown is NOT a line of symmetry?

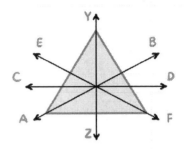

A. AB   C. EF
B. CD   D. ZY

5. Which shape appears to have zero lines of symmetry?

A. 1
B. 2
C. 3
D. 4

6. Which shape appears to have exactly 1 line of symmetry?

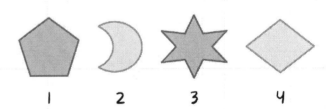

A. 1
B. 2
C. 3
D. 4

7. How many lines of symmetry does this shape have?

A. 2   C. 8
B. 4   D. 16

8. How many lines of symmetry does the letter N have?

A. 4   C. 1
B. 2   D. 0

9. Determine if the line through the figure is a line of symmetry.

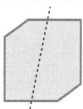

_____

10. Draw all lines of symmetry for this shape.

_____

FITNESS

Please be aware of your environment and be safe at all times. If you cannot do an exercise, just try your best.

Repeat these exercises 4 ROUNDS

1 - Bend forward: 15 times.
Note: try to touch your feet. Make sure to keep your back straight and if needed you can bend your knees.

2 - Lunges: 7 times to each leg.
Note: Use your body weight or books as weight to do leg lunges.

4 - Abs: 15 times

3 - Plank: 20 sec.

Coordinate Plane

Use the graph below to answer questions 1 - 5.

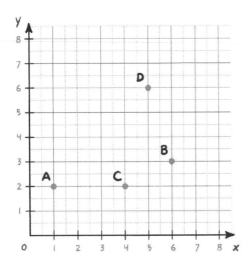

1. What is the x-coordinate for Point D?

   A. 1   C. 5

   B. 4   D. 6

2. What are the coordinates for Point B?

   A. (3, 6)   C. (6, 5)

   B. (2, 6)   D. (6, 3)

3. Which point is located at (5, 6)?

   A. A   C. C

   B. B   D. D

4. Which 2 points have the same y-coordinate?

   A. A and B   C. A and C

   B. B and C   D. C and D

5. What is the y-coordinate for Point B?

   A. 2   C. 4

   B. 3   D. 6

Use the graph below to answer questions 6 - 10.

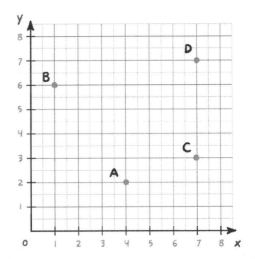

6. What are the coordinates for Point A?

   A. (4, 2)   C. (1, 4)

   B. (7, 3)   D. (4, 6)

7. What is the y-coordinate for Point C?

   A. 1   C. 3

   B. 2   D. 6

8. Which point is located at (1, 6)?

   A. A   C. C

   B. B   D. D

9. Which 2 points have the same x-coordinate?

   A. A and B   C. A and C

   B. B and C   D. C and D

10. What are the coordinates for the origin?

   A. (0, 0)   C. (6, 6)

   B. (1, 1)   D. (7, 7)

The table and the graph below represent 4 flowers in the garden. Use the information to answer questions 11 - 15.

Flower	Point on Graph
tulip	A
peony	B
rose	C
violet	D

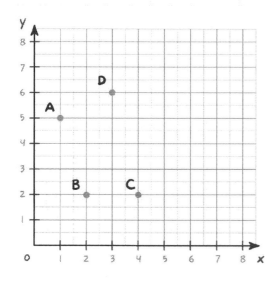

11. Where is the tulip located?

A. (3, 6) C. (1, 5)

B. (6, 3) D. (5, 1)

12. What is the y-coordinate for the rose?

A. 2 C. 5

B. 3 D. 6

13. Which flower is the closest to (3, 6)?

A. Tulip C. Rose

B. Peony D. Violet

14. Which statement is true about a violet and a peony?

A. They have the same y-coordinate.

B. They have the same x-coordinate.

C. The y-coordinate of B is larger than the y-coordinate of D.

D. The x-coordinate of D is larger than the x-coordinate of B.

15. Where is the peony located?

A. (6, 2) C. (2, 6)

B. (2, 2) D. (4, 4)

FITNESS

Please be aware of your environment and be safe at all times. If you cannot do an exercise, just try your best.

Repeat these **exercises** 4 ROUNDS

2 - Chair: 15 sec. Note: sit on an imaginary chair, keep your back straight.

1 - High Plank: 20 sec.

3 - Waist Hooping: 15 times. Note: if you do not have a hoop, pretend you have an imaginary hoop and rotate your hips 10 times.

4 - Abs: 15 times

Classifying 2-d figures

1. If a quadrilateral does not have right angles but two sets of opposite angles that have the same degree and also has 4 sides of equal length, it is a:

A. Rectangle
B. Rhombus
C. Square
D. Trapezoid

2. Which statement is FALSE?

A. All squares have only 1 set of parallel sides.
B. All squares are parallelograms.
C. All squares are rhombuses.
D. All squares have four sides of equal length.

3. Determine which choice best applies to the statement: a quadrilateral has no parallel lines.

A. Rectangle
B. Square
C. Trapezoid
D. None of the above

4. Which statement is true?

A. All rectangles are squares.
B. All rectangles are quadrilaterals.
C. All rectangles have 4 sides that are equal in length.
D. All rectangles have only 1 set of parallel sides.

Use the shapes below to answer questions 5 - 8

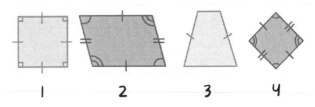

1 2 3 4

5. Which shape is a rhombus?

A. 1   C. 3
B. 2   D. 4

6. Which shape is a square?

A. 1   C. 3
B. 2   D. 4

7. What is the name of shape 2?

_____

8. What is the name of shape 3?

_____

9. A quadrilateral which has 4 angles that are 90° and 4 sides of equal length, is a ...

A. Parallelogram
B. Rectangle
C. Square
D. Trapezoid

10. Which statement is true?

A. All parallelograms have four sides of equal length.
B. All parallelograms are squares.
C. All parallelograms are rhombuses.
D. All parallelograms are quadrilaterals.

11. Which statement is true?

A. A trapezoid has angles which can be of any degree.

B. A trapezoid has **2** sets of parallel sides.

C. All trapezoids have at least one **90°** angle.

D. A trapezoid has **2** sets of perpendicular sides.

12. If a quadrilateral has only one pair of parallel sides, it is a ...

A. Parallelogram

B. Rectangle

C. Square

D. Trapezoid

13. Determine which choice corresponds to this description: a quadrilateral has **4** angles that are **90°**.

A. Parallelogram

B. Rectangle

C. Rhombus

D. Trapezoid

14. Which statement is true?

A. All rhombuses have only I set of equal length sides.

B. All rhombuses are squares.

C. All rhombuses are parallelograms.

D. All rhombuses have only I set of equal angles.

15. Which statement is FALSE?

A. All rectangles are quadrilaterals.

B. All squares are parallelograms.

C. A trapezoid has angles which can be of any degree.

D. All rhombuses are squares.

YOGA

Please be aware of your environment and be safe at all times. If you cannot do an exercise, just try your best.

1 - Down Dog: **25** sec.

2 - Bend Down: **25** sec.

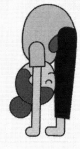

ARCHAEOPTERYx

3 - Chair: **20** sec.

4 - Child Pose: **25** sec.

5 - Shavasana: as long as you can. Note: think of happy moments and relax your mind.

How Environment Affects Plant Growth (Pt. 1)

When you created your food web last week, you saw the crucial role that plants like fruits, grasses, and berries play in an ecosystem. Over the next two weeks, we'll be exploring how environmental factors affect the growth of those plants.

This week, we'll begin by exploring how we can simulate some different environments in our own home. Then, next week, we'll study how our plants held up to the stress test.

Materials:

* I six-pack of small annual flowers (from the nursery or hardware store)
* 6 small pots
* I small bag of sand
* I small bag of potting soil
* An environmental thermometer that can be moved from room to room
* Notepaper

Procedure:

1. Use the environmental thermometer to find three different locations in your house: a place that's consistently normal room temperature (around 70 degrees), a place that's very warm (like an attic or very sunny room), and a place that's very cool (a room in a shady part of the house or maybe a basement). Once you've identified your normal, hot, and cold locations, mark down the temperature that you recorded in each spot on your notepaper.

2. Take one of the small annual flowers and transfer it directly into one of the small pots, adding potting soil as needed. This flower will serve as our **control**, meaning we're not going to mess with it at all.

3. Take two of the flowers and transfer them into two of the small pots. As you put them into the pots, plant them in a mixture that is about **75%** (three quarters) potting soil and about **25%** (one quarter) sand.

4. Take two of the remaining flowers and transfer them into two of the other small pots. As you put them in the pots, plant them in a mixture that's about **50%** (half) potting soil and **50%** (half) sand.

5. Take the final flower and plant it in the final pot, using a mixture that's about **75%** (three quarters) sand and **25%** (one quarter) potting soil.

6. Take your **control** and the **75% sand** plant from Step 5 and put them in the standard, room temperature area that you identified earlier.

7. Take one of the **75%** potting soil plants (from Step 3) and one of the **50%** potting soil plants (from Step 4) and place them in the **cold environment** that you identified earlier.

8. Take one of the **75%** potting soil plants (from Step 3) and one of the **50%** potting soil plants (from Step 4) and place them in the **warm environment** that you identified earlier.

9. On your notepaper, make some predictions about how you think these plants will grow differently based on the temperature, makeup of the soil, and other facts.

10. Over the next week, water these plants the same amount every day or two. You will probably notice that, depending on the soil makeup, some of the plants my struggle to hold the water you give them, but do not provide additional water to those plants. It's important to keep things consistent.

11. Every time you water, bring your notepaper with you and mark down a few observations about how each plant is doing.

Follow-Up Questions:

1. Which flowers do you predict will struggle the most to grow and why?

_____

_____

2. Which factor do you predict is more important to a plant growing effectively: the makeup of the soil or the temperature? What makes you say that?

_____

_____

YOGA

Please be aware of your environment and be safe at all times. If you cannot do an exercise, just try your best.

1 - Tree Pose: Stay as long as possible. Note: do on one leg then on another.

2 - Down Dog: 25 sec.

3 - Stretching: Stay as long as possible. Note: do on one leg then on another.

4 - Lower Plank: 12 sec. Note: Keep your back straight and body tight.

5 - Book Pose: 15 sec. Note: Keep your core tight. Legs should be across from your eyes.

6 - Shavasana: 5 min. Note: this pose is very important and provides you with long term benefits. Try not to skip this. Close your eyes and imagine who you want to be and what your goals are! Always think happy thoughts.

Task: Complete the jigsaw puzzle below. Which piece belongs to which number?

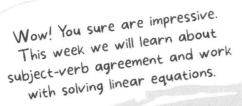

Wow! You sure are impressive. This week we will learn about subject-verb agreement and work with solving linear equations.

WEEK 10

Many of the dinosaur species that were meat eaters walked on two feet making it easier to grab their prey. Dinosaurs that ate plants on the other hand typically walked on four feet.

Subject-Verb Agreement

All nouns and pronouns are regarded as either **singular** or **plural**. That means that there's either one of them (like "apple" or "me") or more than one of them (like "apples" or "us"). In the **present tense** (that is, when a sentence is describing something going on now or something that happens as part of a regular routine), we also have to think about picking a singular or plural **verb**. When you use a singular noun, it's also important to use a singular verb. When you use a plural noun, it's important to use a **plural verb**. We call this concept **subject-verb agreement.**

For native English speakers, subject-verb agreement errors are usually easy to **hear** when people make them out loud, but they can be tougher to **see** when they're written on the page. That's why you need to know what to look for!

Key Terms

Singular Noun: A noun that represents one person, place, thing, or idea

❋ Car, Hat, Bird, Pony, etc.

Plural Noun: A noun that represents more than one person, place, thing, or idea

❋ Cars, Hats, Birds, Ponies, etc.

Collective Noun: A noun that represents a group of objects acting as one unit

❋ A **team** of athletes, a **flock** of birds, a **class** of students, etc.

Hint:

When it comes to detecting subject-verb agreement errors, one of the best strategies is to **try saying it out loud!** Like we said before, subject-verb agreement errors are easier to **hear** than they are to see! That means that, if it doesn't sound right, it probably isn't right!

For Example...

❋ The dogs walk across the street.
❋ The dog walks across the street.

* The **plural noun** "dogs" takes the **plural verb** "walk"
* The **singular noun** "dog" takes the **singular verb** "walks"

❋ The dogs walked across the street.
❋ The dog walked across the street.

* As you can see, there are **no singular or plural verbs in the past tense!**

❋ Frank always **eats** eggs for breakfast.
❋ Frank and Katarina always **eat** eggs for breakfast.

* The **singular** subject "Frank" takes the **singular verb** "eats"
* The **plural** subject "Frank and Katarina" takes the **plural verb** "eat"

❋ The hockey <u>team</u> always **eats** eggs for breakfast.

* Here, you see an example of a **collective noun.** The hockey **team** clearly contains more than one person, but those people **act as one unit.** Therefore, collective nouns like "team" or "class" always take **singular verbs** because they act as **one unit.**

From "The Raven"

By Edgar Allan Poe

Once upon a midnight dreary, while I pondered, weak and weary,
Over many a quaint and curious volume of forgotten lore—
While I nodded, nearly napping, suddenly there came a tapping,
As of some one gently rapping, rapping at my chamber door.
"'Tis some visitor," I muttered, "tapping at my chamber door—
Only this and nothing more."

Ah, distinctly I remember it was in the bleak December;
And each separate dying ember wrought its ghost upon the floor.
Eagerly I wished the morrow;—vainly I had sought to borrow

From my books surcease of sorrow—sorrow for the lost Lenore—
For the rare and radiant maiden whom the angels name Lenore—
Nameless here for evermore.

And the silken, sad, uncertain rustling of each purple curtain
Thrilled me—filled me with fantastic terrors never felt before;
So that now, to still the beating of my heart, I stood repeating
"'Tis some visitor entreating entrance at my chamber door—
Some late visitor entreating entrance at my chamber door;—
This it is and nothing more."

Presently my soul grew stronger; hesitating then no longer,
"Sir," said I, "or Madam, truly your forgiveness I implore;
But the fact is I was napping, and so gently you came rapping,
And so faintly you came tapping, tapping at my chamber door,
That I scarce was sure I heard you"—here I opened wide the door;—
Darkness there and nothing more.

1. Based on the text of the poem, where does this story take place? What words or lines provided you with hints?

_____

_____

2. What can we **infer** or guess about Lenore? What relationship does it seem Lenore had to the narrator?

_____

_____

3. What noise does the narrator fixate on throughout the passage?

   A. The crowing of a raven
   B. A light knocking on his door
   C. The cries of his lost Lenore
   D. The sound of total silence

4. Why is **subject-verb agreement** <u>not</u> a major issue in this poem?

   A. Because all the singular subjects have singular verbs and all the plural subjects have plural verbs
   B. Because subject-verb agreement doesn't matter in poetry
   C. Because the poem is written in the past tense
   D. Because there are no verbs in the poem

5. How do the events of the final **stanza** (grouping of lines) represent a twist or reversal from what came before?

_____

_____

_____

_____

Identifying Subject-Verb Agreement Errors

Directions: Read each sentence below and determine whether it contains any subject-verb agreement errors. If the sentence is grammatically correct, write **correct** on the line below. If the sentence contains a subject-verb agreement error, write **incorrect** on the line below, <u>cross out the incorrect verb,</u> and, using your pen, write the correct verb above it.

1. It's not fair that Maurice and John always gets all the attention.

_____

2. Of my two dogs, Bailey is the one who requires more attention, while Bandit are much more of a pleasure to deal with.

_____

3. "If anyone stand up before I dismiss you, that person will get detention," Ms. Facione warned.

_____

4. The team always eat a healthy meal as a group before getting on the bus and heading to a game.

_____

5. The members of the team always eat a healthy meal as a group before getting on the bus and heading to a game.

_____

FITNESS

Today you get to decide what fitness activity you would like to do!

From "The Raven"

By Edgar Allan Poe

(Continued from Day One's Passage)

Deep into that darkness peering, long I stood there wondering, fearing,
Doubting, dreaming dreams no mortal ever dared to dream before;
But the silence was unbroken, and the stillness gave no token,
And the only word there spoken was the whispered word, "Lenore?"
This I whispered, and an echo murmured back the word, "Lenore!"—
Merely this and nothing more.

Back into the chamber turning, all my soul within me burning,
Soon again I heard a tapping somewhat louder than before.
"Surely," said I, "surely that is something at my window lattice;
Let me see, then, what thereat is, and this mystery explore—
Let my heart be still a moment and this mystery explore;—
'Tis the wind and nothing more!"

Open here I flung the shutter, when, with many a flirt and flutter,
In there stepped a stately Raven of the saintly days of yore;
Not the least obeisance made he; not a minute stopped or stayed he;
But, with mien of lord or lady, perched above my chamber door—
Perched upon a bust of Pallas just above my chamber door—
Perched, and sat, and nothing more.

Then this ebony bird beguiling my sad fancy into smiling,
By the grave and stern decorum of the countenance it wore,
"Though thy crest be shorn and shaven, thou," I said, "art sure no craven,
Ghastly grim and ancient Raven wandering from the Nightly shore—
Tell me what thy lordly name is on the Night's Plutonian shore!"
Quoth the Raven "Nevermore."

Much I marvelled this ungainly fowl to hear discourse so plainly,
Though its answer little meaning—little relevancy bore;
For we cannot help agreeing that no living human being
Ever yet was blessed with seeing bird above his chamber door—
Bird or beast upon the sculptured bust above his chamber door,
With such name as "Nevermore."

1. Why is the narrator feeling creeped out at the beginning of this passage? (**Note:** It may be useful to review the Day One passage as well!)

_____

_____

2. How does the raven get into the room with the narrator?

_____

_____

3. How is the **raven** described at first?

    A. Loud and scary
    B. Ugly and dirty
    C. Confused and injured
    D. Distinguished and honorable

4. What assumption does the narrator make when the raven speaks?

    A. That it is magical
    B. That it represents his lost Lenore
    C. That its name is "Nevermore"
    D. That he is dreaming

5. **Why** do you think the narrator is so fascinated by the raven? Why would it be so important to him?

_____

_____

_____

_____

_____

Creating Subject-Verb Agreement

Directions: Each sentence below contains a blank where either a **noun** (person, place, thing, or idea) or **verb** (an action or state of being) needs to go. Brainstorm a word that could appropriately fill that blank and write it down on the line. Be sure that your word creates a **present-tense sentence** in which the subject and verb agree.

1. We always _____ a camping trip in the early fall. (VERB)

2. When _____ swim underwater, they have a graceful, playful appearance. (NOUN)

3. My brother _____ and _____ in his sleep every night. (TWO VERBS)

4. _____ tend to do better on quizzes and tests before lunch. (NOUN)

5. When the wind _____ through the leaves, it makes a beautiful, peaceful sound. (VERB)

FITNESS

Please be aware of your environment and be safe at all times. If you cannot do an exercise, just try your best.

Repeat these **exercises 4 ROUNDS**

2 - Side Bending: 10 times to each side. Note: try to touch your feet.

3 - Tree Pose: Stay as long as possible. Note: do the same with the other leg.

1 - Squats: 15 times. Note: imagine you are trying to sit on a chair.

Solving and writing equations

1. What is the solution to this equation: $25 + x = 32$?

   A. $x = 4$ C. $x = 6$

   B. $x = 5$ D. $x = 7$

2. Solve the problem $a + 15 = 43$.

   A. $a = 26$ C. $a = 28$

   B. $a = 27$ D. $a = 29$

3. What is y in the equation $4y = 68$?

   A. $y = 16$ C. $y = 18$

   B. $y = 17$ D. $y = 19$

4. Find a solution for the problem $1\frac{2}{6} + c = 3\frac{5}{12}$.

   A. $2\frac{1}{12}$ C. $1\frac{5}{12}$

   B. $2\frac{1}{6}$ D. $1\frac{2}{6}$

5. What is the solution to this equation $k + \frac{3}{5} = \frac{8}{10}$?

   A. $\frac{1}{10}$ C. $\frac{2}{5}$

   B. $\frac{3}{10}$ D. $\frac{1}{5}$

6. There are 120 students in 5 classrooms. If the students are dispersed evenly among the classrooms, which equation could be used to find the number of students, x, in one classroom?

   A. $x + 5 = 120$

   B. $x - 5 = 120$

   C. $x \times 5 = 120$

   D. $x \div 5 = 120$

7. There are a total of 108 toys in boxes. Each box has 18 toys in it. Which equation could be used to find the total number of boxes, y?

   A. $18y = 108$

   B. $18 + y = 108$

   C. $18 \div y = 108$

   D. $108 - y = 18$

8. Daniel practiced math for $2\frac{1}{4}$ hours on Monday. On Tuesday he practiced x hours more than on Monday. Which equation could be used to find how much longer Daniel practiced on Tuesday if he practiced a total of $3\frac{1}{2}$ hours on Tuesday?

   A. $2\frac{1}{4} \times x = 3\frac{1}{2}$

   B. $2\frac{1}{4} \div x = 3\frac{1}{2}$

   C. $2\frac{1}{4} + x = 3\frac{1}{2}$

   D. $2\frac{1}{4} - x = 3\frac{1}{2}$

9. There is a total of 224 pounds of flour in bags. One bag of flour weighs 32 pounds. Write an equation that could be used to find the total number of bags of flour and find a solution to the equation.

10. There are 264 kilograms of apples at the store. They are evenly distributed into 12 boxes. Which equation could be used to find the amount of apples, k, in one box?

   A. $k = 264 - 12$

   B. $k = 264 + 12$

   C. $k = 264 \times 12$

   D. $k = 264 \div 12$

175

David ran $1\frac{1}{4}$ miles. Joseph ran x miles. Together they ran $1\frac{1}{2}$ miles. Use this information to answer questions 11 - 12.

11. Which equation could be used to find how far Joseph ran?

A. $1\frac{1}{2} + x = 1\frac{1}{4}$

B. $1\frac{1}{2} - x = 1\frac{1}{4}$

C. $1\frac{1}{2} \times x = 1\frac{1}{4}$

D. $1\frac{1}{2} \div x = 1\frac{1}{4}$

12. How many miles did Joseph run?

A. $\frac{1}{2}$ miles

B. $\frac{3}{4}$ miles

C. $\frac{2}{4}$ miles

D. $\frac{1}{4}$ miles

Olivia spent \$13.5 on 3 boxes of pencils. The variable "a" represents one box of pencils. Use this information to answer questions 13 - 14.

13. Which equation could be used to find the cost of 1 box of pencils?

A. $a \times 13.5 = 3$

B. $a \div 13.5 = 3$

C. $3a = 13.5$

D. $13.5 - a = 3$

14. What was the cost of one box of pencils?

A. \$4.20

B. \$4.30

C. \$4.45

D. \$4.50

15. What is the solution to this equation $35 + y = 79$?

_____

16. Find a solution for the problem $56 \div x = 8$.

_____

FITNESS

Please be aware of your environment and be safe at all times. If you cannot do an exercise, just try your best.

Repeat these exercises 4 ROUNDS

2 - Lunges: 7 times to each leg.
Note: Use your body weight or books as weight to do leg lunges.

1 - Bend forward: 15 times.
Note: try to touch your feet. Make sure to keep your back straight and if needed you can bend your knees.

4 - Abs: 15 times

3 - Plank: 20 sec.

Area of triangles

1. Find the area of the triangle.

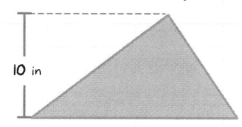

10 in

18 in

A. 45 sq in   C. 145 sq in
B. 90 sq in   D. 180 sq in

2. What is the area of the triangle?

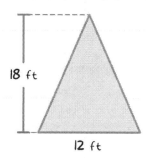

18 ft

12 ft

A. 86 sq ft   C. 98 sq ft
B. 88 sq ft   D. 108 sq ft

3. Find the area of the triangle.

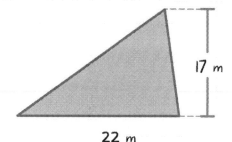

17 m

22 m

A. 157 sq m
B. 174 sq m
C. 187 sq m
D. 194 sq m

4. What is the area of the triangle?

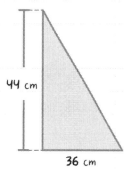

44 cm

36 cm

A. 672 sq cm   C. 812 sq cm
B. 792 sq cm   D. 862 sq cm

5. What is the area of the shaded triangle?

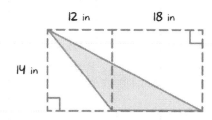

12 in   18 in

14 in

A. 126 sq in   C. 232 sq in
B. 156 sq in   D. 252 sq in

6. The base of the triangle is 16 cm and the height of the triangle is 8 cm. What is the area of this triangle?

7. What is the area of the shaded part?

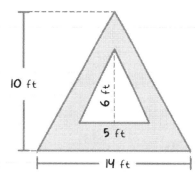

10 ft

6 ft

5 ft

14 ft

A. 49 sq ft   C. 64 sq ft
B. 55 sq ft   D. 74 sq ft

8. What is the area of the shape?

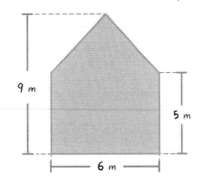

9 m

5 m

6 m

A. 34 sq m   C. 42 sq m

B. 38 sq m   D. 45 sq m

9. Find the area of the right triangle below.

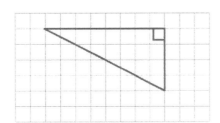

A. 16 square units

B. 24 square units

C. 28 square units

D. 32 square units

10. What is the area of the triangle?

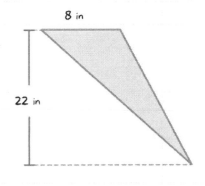

8 in

22 in

11. Find the area of the shaded part.

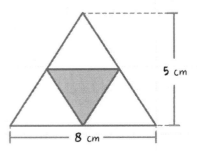

5 cm

8 cm

12. The base of the triangle is **25** yd and the height of the triangle is **7** yd. What is the area of this triangle?

FITNESS

Please be aware of your environment and be safe at all times. If you cannot do an exercise, just try your best.

Repeat these **exercises 4 ROUNDS**

2 - Chair: 15 sec.
Note: sit on an imaginary chair, keep your back straight.

1 - High Plank: 20 sec.

3 - Waist Hooping: 15 times. Note: if you do not have a hoop, pretend you have an imaginary hoop and rotate your hips 10 times.

4 - Abs: 15 times

Division Problems

1. Find $1,035 \div 23$

   A. 55
   B. 45
   C. 35
   D. 25

2. Find the divider of 952 to get 68.

   A. 14
   B. 19
   C. 24
   D. 27

3. How many times is the number 22 less than the number 7,634?

   A. 442
   B. 417
   C. 372
   D. 347

4. Which number sentence below is true?

   A. $5,264 \div 16 = 329$
   B. $2,652 \div 34 = 88$
   C. $2,205 \div 45 = 59$
   D. $5,335 \div 55 = 87$

5. What is the quotient when 6,758 is divided by 26?

   A. 268 r 18
   B. 259 r 24
   C. 254 r 16
   D. 335 r 21

6. What is $5,376 \div 42$?

   A. 128
   B. 126
   C. 127
   D. 125

7. How many times is the number 27 less than the number 2,538?

   A. 96
   B. 94
   C. 88
   D. 84

8. What is the remainder when 6,732 is divided by 35?

   A. 10
   B. 12
   C. 18
   D. 24

9. What is the quotient when 9,724 is divided by 43?

   A. 216 r 16
   B. 234 r 28
   C. 226 r 6
   D. 265 r 37

10. What is $6,804 \div 21$?

   A. 324
   B. 344
   C. 364
   D. 374

11. Determine the missing remainder for the problem.

$$1,638 \div 24 = 68 \text{ r} \underline{\hspace{2cm}}$$

12. What is the missing number in the equation $3,008 \div \underline{\hspace{2cm}} = 64$?

13. Determine the number that correctly fills in the blank. $\underline{\hspace{2cm}} \div 62 = 37$.

14. What is $2,028 \div 26$?

15. Which number sentence below is FALSE?

A. $2,380 \div 68 = 35$
B. $3,402 \div 42 = 81$
C. $2,159 \div 71 = 29$
D. $2,430 \div 54 = 45$

16. Find $4,514 \div 74$.

17. Determine the missing remainder for the problem.

$$5,933 \div 64 = 92 \text{ r} \underline{\hspace{2cm}}$$

18. Solve the problem: $3,402 \div 14 =$

19. What is the missing number in the equation: $2,842 \div \underline{\hspace{2cm}} = 58$

20. Determine the number that correctly fills in the blank. $5,568 \div \underline{\hspace{2cm}} = 87$.

FITNESS

Please be aware of your environment and be safe at all times. If you cannot do an exercise, just try your best.

Repeat these
exercises
4 ROUNDS

3 - Lunges: 7 times to each leg.
Note: Use your body weight or books as weight to do leg lunges.

1 - Bend forward: 15 times.
Note: try to touch your feet. Make sure to keep your back straight and if needed you can bend your knees.

2 - Plank: 20 sec.

WEEK 10
DAY 6 EXPERIMENT

How Environment Affects Plant Growth (Pt. 2)

Last week, we planted some flowers in a variety of different conditions to see how differences in environment affect plant growth. This week, we'll check back in with our plants to study them carefully and see how some drastic differences in environment have impacted their ability to grow.

Materials:

* Your 6 potted flowers from the Week 9 experiment
* Notepaper (with your observations from throughout the last week)
* A plastic trash bag
* A ruler or tape measure
* Magnifying glass (optional)

Procedure:

1. Gather your 6 potted plants throughout the house. Make sure you label each one so you don't mix up which ones grew with the different temperatures and soil mixtures.

2. Open up your trash bag so that it can be laid flat. You can cut the bag to make it easier, if you'd like. Cover your work surface (table, floor, etc.) with the trash bag. (This is to prevent us from getting dirt everywhere!)

3. Using your ruler or tape measure, measure the height of each plant and mark them down on your note sheet.

4. Next examine each plant closely using your eyes. A magnifying glass can be extremely useful for this work. Make note of the relative colors of the plants. Check to see which ones have stems and leaves that feel the sturdiest. Inspect to see which plants still have healthy flowers on them. Describe the condition of each plant in your notes.

5. Next, carefully pull the flowers out of their pots one at a time over the trash bag to keep things neat. Carefully examine the roots that the flower has formed in the soil. You can measure their length using your ruler, if you want. Try to see how strong or healthy the roots appear, and make note of that (if you want to keep one of your flowers, it's best to save the control plant).

6. After you've completed your notes, carefully dispose of the flowers you're not keeping and any leftover dirt or sand.

7. Review your notes carefully and look for trends: How did the quality of the flowers change with different levels of sand? Which temperature seemed to work best? Take some time to think about what the data is telling you.

Follow-Up Questions:

1. How did the addition of **sand** to the soil impact the flowers' abilities to grow?

_____

_____

_____

2. How did the variations in **temperature** impact the flowers' abilities to grow?

_____

_____

_____

YOGA

Please be aware of your environment and be safe at all times. If you cannot do an exercise, just try your best.

1 - Tree Pose: Stay as long as possible. Note: do on one leg then on another.

2 - Down Dog: 25 sec.

3 - Stretching: Stay as long as possible. Note: do on one leg then on another.

5 - Book Pose: 15 sec. Note: Keep your core tight. Legs should be across from your eyes.

4 - Lower Plank: 12 sec. Note: Keep your back straight and body tight.

6 - Shavasana: 5 min. Note: this pose is very important and provides you with long term benefits. Try not to skip this. Close your eyes and imagine who you want to be and what your goals are! Always think happy thoughts.

Task: Color in a path that leads to the castle.

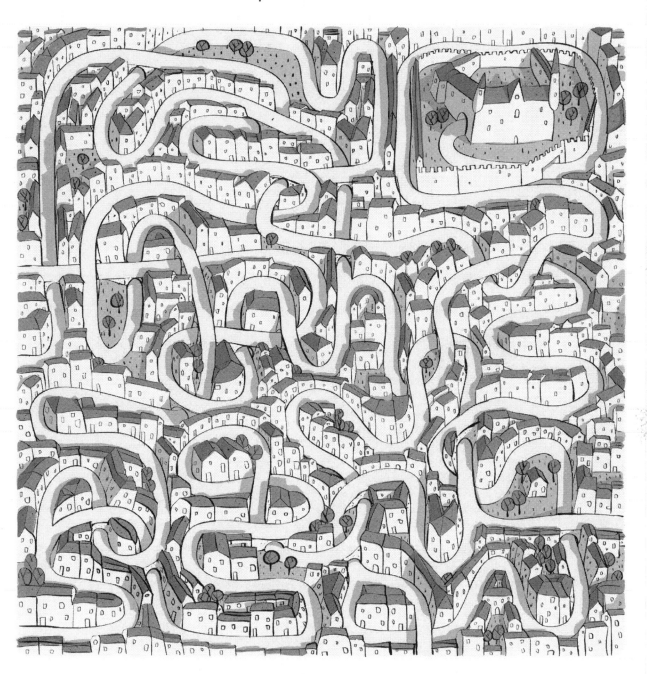

OVERVIEW OF ENGLISH CONCEPTS

Active vs. Passive Voice

Now that you're familiar with the building blocks of sentence structure, it's time to make sure we're writing **the best possible sentences**, not just sentences that are grammatically correct. Part of writing the **best** possible sentences is knowing the difference between **active voice** and **passive voice.**

Active voice occurs when the **subject** of the sentence is the one **doing or performing** the action of the main verb. **Passive voice** occurs when the subject of the sentence is having the action of the main verb **done or performed to it.** Generally speaking, most writers agree that **active voice** is always preferable in formal writing, because it is more clear for the reader and cuts down on unnecessary wordiness.

Identifying Active Voice:

Active voice occurs when the **subject of the sentence** is doing or performing the verb.

* **Stan** flew a kite in the wind yesterday.
  * The subject (Stan) is the one who performed the action (flew the kite).
* **The kitty** lapped up the milk from its bowl.
  * The subject (the kitty) is the one who performed the action (lapped up the milk).
* **Marty and Gene** fought for hours over who was right and who was wrong.
  * The subject (Marty and Gene) are the ones who performed the action (fought).

Identifying Passive Voice:

Passive voice occurs when the **subject of the sentence** is not doing or performing the action of the verb. In most cases, it is having action performed on or to it.

* The **ball** was kicked by a screaming student.
  * Is the subject (ball) the one kicking anything?
    * No! The subject is being kicked. That's passive voice!
* **Jennifer** got yelled at by the librarian for having her phone out during study hall.
  * Is the subject (Jennifer) the one yelling at anyone?
    * No! The subject is being yelled at. That's passive voice!
* The **milk** in the bowl was lapped up by the kitty.
  * Is the subject (milk) the one lapping anything?
    * No! The subject is being lapped up. That's passive voice!

Hint:

When you're not sure if a sentence is written in the **active** or **passive** voice, try isolating the **simple subject** and the **simple predicate** (verb). If you can isolate those two words and determine if the **simple subject** is performing the **simple predicate**, then you'll know what kind of voice you're dealing with!

From "Dracula"

By Bram Stoker

Suddenly, I became conscious of the fact that the driver was in the act of pulling up the horses in the courtyard of a vast ruined castle, from whose tall black windows came no ray of light, and whose broken battlements showed a jagged line against the moonlit sky.

I must have been asleep, for certainly if I had been fully awake I must have noticed the approach of such a remarkable place. In the gloom the courtyard looked of considerable size, and as several dark ways led from it under great round arches, it perhaps seemed bigger than it really is. I have not yet been able to see it by daylight.

When the coach stopped, the driver jumped down and held out his hand to assist me to alight. Again I could not but notice his prodigious strength. His hand actually seemed like a steel vice that could have crushed mine if he had chosen. Then he took out my traps, and placed them on the ground beside me as I stood close to a great door, old and studded with large iron nails, and set in a projecting doorway of massive stone. I could see even in the dim light that the stone was massively carved, but that the carving had been much worn by time and weather. As I stood, the driver jumped again into his seat and shook the reins; the horses started forward, and trap and all disappeared down one of the dark openings.

I stood in silence where I was, for I did not know what to do. Of bell or knocker there was no sign; through these frowning walls and dark window openings it was not likely that my voice could penetrate. The time I waited seemed endless, and I felt doubts and fears crowding upon me. What sort of place had I come to, and among what kind of people? What sort of grim adventure was it on which I had embarked? Was this a customary incident in the life of a solicitor's clerk sent out to explain the purchase of a London estate to a foreigner? Solicitor's clerk! Mina would not like that. Solicitor—for just before leaving London I got word that my examination was successful; and I am now a full-blown solicitor! I began to rub my eyes and pinch myself to see if I were awake. It all seemed like a horrible nightmare to me, and I expected that I should suddenly awake, and find myself at home, with the dawn struggling in through the windows, as I had now and again felt in the morning after a day of overwork. But my flesh answered the pinching test, and my eyes were not to be deceived. I was indeed awake and in Romania. All I could do now was to be patient, and to wait the coming of the morning.

1. Describe the castle where the narrator arrives in your own words:

_____

_____

2. Name at least **two things** that seem strange about the carriage driver:

_____

_____

3. What feeling does the narrator experience throughout the passage?

    A. He feels like someone is watching him

    B. He feels like he must be dreaming

    C. He feels like he is in an evil place

    D. He feels like something bad is happening back at his home

4. What strategies does the narrator use to make sure what he is experiencing is real?

    A. He pinches himself and rubs his eyes

    B. He repeatedly tells himself to wake up

    C. He asks the other characters for help

    D. He focuses on being patient with himself and his surroundings

5. How do the **plot details, characters, and setting** all contribute to the dark or ominous tone of this passage?

_____

_____

_____

_____

_____

Active vs. Passive Voice

Directions: Read each sentence and, on the line below, identify whether it is written in the active or passive voice. After you've made your decision, write a sentence explaining how you know your answer is right.

1. Our mailbox got knocked over by a snowplow last winter.

This sentence is in the _____ voice. I know that because

_____

_____

2. The dog almost pulled my arm out of its socket by yanking on the leash.

This sentence is in the _____ voice. I know that because

_____

_____

3. This area gets hit by a hurricane every couple of years.

This sentence is in the _____ voice. I know that because

_____

_____

4. Let's build a kite so we can study the wind and have fun at the same time!

This sentence is in the _____ voice. I know that because

_____

_____

5. My nails always wind up getting bitten in situations where I'm nervous or scared.

This sentence is in the _____ voice. I know that because

_____

_____

Today you get to decide what fitness activity you would like to do!

From "Dracula"

By Bram Stoker

(Continued from Day One's Passage)

"I heard a heavy step approaching behind the great door, and saw through the chinks the gleam of a coming light. Then there was the sound of rattling chains and the clanking of massive bolts drawn back. A key was turned with the loud grating noise of long disuse, and the great door swung back.

Within, stood a tall old man, clean shaven save for a long white moustache, and clad in black from head to foot, without a single speck of colour about him anywhere. He held in his hand an antique silver lamp, in which the flame burned without chimney or globe of any kind, throwing long quivering shadows as it flickered in the draught of the open door. The old man motioned me in with his right hand with a courtly gesture, saying in excellent English, but with a strange intonation:—

"Welcome to my house! Enter freely and of your own will!" He made no motion of stepping to meet me, but stood like a statue, as though his gesture of welcome had fixed him into stone. The instant, however, that I had stepped over the threshold, he moved impulsively forward, and holding out his hand grasped mine with a strength which made me wince, an effect which was not lessened by the fact that it seemed as cold as ice—more like the hand of a dead than a living man. Again he said:—

"Welcome to my house. Come freely. Go safely; and leave something of the happiness you bring!" The strength of the handshake was so much akin to that which I had noticed in the driver, whose face I had not seen, that for a moment I doubted if it were not the same person to whom I was speaking; so to make sure, I said interrogatively:—

"Count Dracula?" He bowed in a courtly way as he replied:—

"I am Dracula; and I bid you welcome, Mr. Harker, to my house. Come in; the night air is chill, and you must need to eat and rest." As he was speaking, he put the lamp on a bracket on the wall, and stepping out, took my luggage; he had carried it in before I could forestall him. I protested but he insisted:—

"Nay, sir, you are my guest. It is late, and my people are not available. Let me see to your comfort myself."

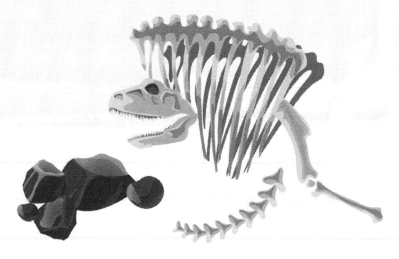

1. Describe the **tone** and **mood** of this passage. How are the setting and the characters presented, and what emotional response or feelings does that create for the reader?

_____

_____

2. Why does the lamp that Dracula carries contribute to the creepiness of the scene?

_____

_____

3. What does Count Dracula have in common with the carriage driver from Day One's passage?

   A. He is very helpful
   B. He has a mustache
   C. He is very strong
   D. He is very friendly

4. What makes the narrator say that Count Dracula seems more like a dead man than a living one?

   A. He is very old
   B. He lives in a creepy castle
   C. He seems to be very frail
   D. He has extremely cold hands

5. How is Count Dracula's appearance, behavior, or attitude **strange** or **unusual?** What stands out to you from the passage? (Provide **at least** four details.)

_____

_____

_____

_____

_____

Transforming Passive Voice

Directions: Each sentence below is written in the passive voice. Generally, writers and editors try to focus on using the active voice because it allows them to writer stronger, clearer sentences. Read each sentence; then, on the lines below, rewrite it in the active voice, so that the subject of the sentence is performing the action of the verb.

1.   The massive web in the corner of our kitchen was woven by a careful, cunning spider

   _____

   _____

2.   My cousin Corey got picked in the third round of the professional football draft by a team in Texas.

   _____

   _____

3.   The United States Postal Service is considered by many Americans to be the most important service in our country.

   _____

   _____

4.   Early yesterday morning, my car was stolen by some kind of a thief while I was sleeping.

   _____

   _____

5.   That home run by Juan Cabrera was hit so hard that, if it wasn't for the scoreboard, it would've gone out of the stadium.

   _____

   _____

FITNESS

Please be aware of your environment and be safe at all times. If you cannot do an exercise, just try your best.

1 - Squats: 15 times. Note: imagine you are trying to sit on a chair.

2 - Side Bending: 10 times to each side. Note: try to touch your feet.

3 - Tree Pose: Stay as long as possible. Note: do the same with the other leg.

Ratios and rates

Below are the number of 4 types of trees in the garden. Use this table below to answer questions 1 - 4

Apple trees	54
Pear trees	36
Plum trees	12
Apricot trees	18

1. What is the ratio of pear trees to apricot trees?

A. 6 : 2   C. 3 : 1
B. 6 : 1   D. 2 : 1

2. What is the ratio of apple trees to plum trees?

A. 3 : 2   C. 9 : 2
B. 9 : 6   D. 6 : 2

3. What is the ratio of pear trees to apple trees?

A. 3 : 4   C. 3 : 6
B. 2 : 3   D. 5 : 6

4. What is the ratio of plum trees to apricot trees?

A. 1 : 3   C. 2 : 3
B. 3 : 6   D. 4 : 6

5. What is the ratio of apple trees to all the trees in the garden?

A. 6 : 10   C. 3 : 12
B. 9 : 20   D. 6 : 18

6. What is the ratio of stars to circles?

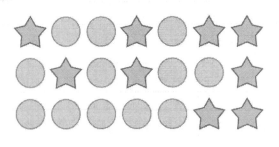

A. 1 : 2
B. 3 : 4
C. 4 : 3
D. 6 : 9

7. The ratio of dogs to cats is 2 : 5. If there are 4 dogs, how many cats are there?

A. 8
B. 10
C. 15
D. 20

8. What is the ratio of triangles to squares?

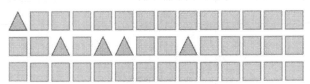

9. There were 24 big boxes for every 21 small boxes. What is the ratio of big boxes to small boxes?

10. The ratio of roses to all flowers in the garden is 3 : 7. If there are 27 roses, how many flowers are in the garden?

11. Mr. Williams used 4 yards of a board to make 3 benches. How many yards of the board did he use for each bench?

A. $\frac{5}{3}$ yards   C. $1\frac{2}{3}$ yards

B. $1\frac{1}{3}$ yards   D. $\frac{2}{3}$ yards

12. Luke earned $32 for washing 4 cars. How much did Luke earn per car?

13. Scarlet spent $24.75 on three T-shirts. What is the cost of seven T-shirts?

A. $49.75   C. $55.65

B. $53.25   D. $57.75

14. The ratio of trucks to all cars in the parking lot is 2:5. If there are 14 trucks, how many cars are there in total in the parking lot?

15. Owen worked for 12 hours and earned $72. How much did Owen earn per hour?

16. Mrs. Bell purchased 4 packages of potatoes for $14. Each package was 5 pounds. How much would she pay for 1 pound of potatoes?

A. $1   C. $0.75

B. $0.80   D. $0.70

17. If 9 pies used 45 ounces of flour, how many ounces of flour are in 4 pies?

18. Evelyn spent 4 days solving math problems. During this time she solved a total of 72 problems. If she solves problems at a constant rate, how many problems would Evelyn have solved in just 2 days?

A. 18   C. 36

B. 27   D. 42

FITNESS

Please be aware of your environment and be safe at all times. If you cannot do an exercise, just try your best.

Repeat these **exercises** **4 ROUNDS**

2 - Lunges: 7 times to each leg.
Note: Use your body weight or books as weight to do leg lunges.

1 - Bend forward: 15 times.
Note: try to touch your feet. Make sure to keep your back straight and if needed you can bend your knees.

4 - Abs: 15 times

3 - Plank: 20 sec.

Angles (Right Angles, Acute Angles, Obtuse Angles) and finding angles of shapes

1. Is this angle less than, equal to, or greater than a right angle?

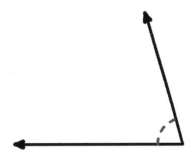

2. Tick the boxes that could be applied to each angle.

Angle	Acute	Obtuse	Right

3. Identify each angle of the shape below. (Acute, Obtuse, or Right)

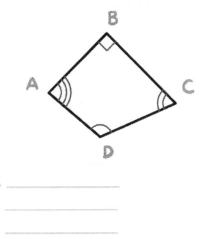

A _____

B _____

C _____

D _____

4. For the shape below, count the number of angles of each type.

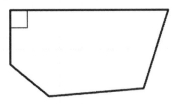

Number of acute angles _____

Number of obtuse angles _____

Number of right angles _____

5. What is the measurement of this angle? Choose the best estimate.

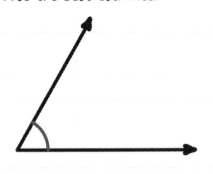

A. 30°   C. 60°

B. 45°   D. 90°

194

6. Classify each angle as acute, obtuse, or right.

10° _____

110° _____

45° _____

135° _____

Use the shapes below to answer questions 8 - 10.

7. Look at the angle marked on this shape:

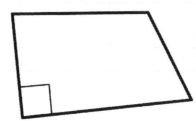

What type of angle is it?

A. Acute

B. Obtuse

C. Right

D. None of the above

8. Count the total number of acute angles inside the shapes.

_____

9. Count the total number of obtuse angles inside the shapes.

_____

10. Count the total number of right angles inside the shapes.

_____

FITNESS

Please be aware of your environment and be safe at all times. If you cannot do an exercise, just try your best.

Repeat these **exercises 4 ROUNDS**

2 - Chair: 15 sec.
Note: sit on an imaginary chair, keep your back straight.

4 - Abs:
15 times

3 - Waist Hooping: 15 times. Note: if you do not have a hoop, pretend you have an imaginary hoop and rotate your hips 10 times.

1 - High Plank:
20 sec.

195

Greatest Common Factor / Least Common Multiple

1. What is the greatest common factor of 20 and 45?

   A. 1
   B. 4
   C. 5
   D. 9

2. What is the least common multiple of 5 and 11?

   A. 122
   B. 110
   C. 60
   D. 55

3. What is the greatest common factor of 6 and 33?

   A. 2
   B. 3
   C. 6
   D. 11

4. Find the least common multiple of 2 and 9.

   A. 9
   B. 18
   C. 36
   D. 48

5. Determine the greatest common factor of 22 and 30.

   A. 15
   B. 11
   C. 3
   D. 2

6. Determine the least common multiple of 8 and 10.

   A. 32
   B. 40
   C. 80
   D. 88

7. What is the greatest common factor of 16 and 24?

   A. 2
   B. 4
   C. 8
   D. 12

8. What is the least common multiple of 7 and 8?

   A. 35
   B. 40
   C. 49
   D. 56

9. Determine the greatest common factor of 56 and 63.

   A. 9
   B. 8
   C. 7
   D. 4

10. Find the least common multiple of 12 and 4.

    A. 48
    B. 36
    C. 24
    D. 12

11. What is the greatest common factor of 12 and 39?

    A. 1   C. 12
    B. 3   D. 39

12. Determine the least common multiple of 9 and 3?

   A. 63   C. 9

   B. 27   D. 3

13. Determine the greatest common factor of 18 and 30.

   A. 1   C. 3

   B. 2   D. 18

14. Find the least common multiple of 10 and 12?

   A. 120   C. 24

   B. 60   D. 12

15. What is the greatest common factor of 36 and 12?

   A. 3

   B. 4

   C. 6

   D. 12

16. What is the least common multiple of 4 and 7?

_____

17. What is the greatest common factor of 96 and 18?

   A. 8   C. 3

   B. 6   D. 2

18. What is the greatest common factor of 6 and 15?

_____

19. Find the greatest common factor of 24 and 20.

_____

20. Which expression is equivalent to 25 + 15?

   A. $5(5 + 3)$

   B. $2(5 + 15)$

   C. $(2 + 3) \times 5$

   D. $5(2 + 1)$

YOGA

Please be aware of your environment and be safe at all times. If you cannot do an exercise, just try your best.

1 - Down Dog: 25 sec.

2 - Bend Down: 25 sec.

3 - Chair: 20 sec.

5 - Shavasana: as long as you can. Note: think of happy moments and relax your mind.

4 - Child Pose: 25 sec.

Observing Rocks and Minerals

In the 21st century, most of us live lives where we don't think about rocks every day. With that said, rocks and minerals are as crucial to our lives here on Earth as water, trees, or any other natural features. Today, we will gather some of the different rocks and minerals that occur in your local area and study them to see what we can learn!

Materials:

* An assortment of rocks or stones from your area (see Step 1 below)
* A magnifying glass
* A kitchen scale
* A ruler or tape measure
* A sink with running water
* Paper towel
* Notepaper
* An encyclopedia or internet access for research
* A piece of cement (such as an outdoor step or basement floor — optional)

Procedure:

1. Start by taking a nice walk in your local area. It could be at a park, in the woods, or wherever you can be near nature. As you walk, try to pick up at least 10 different rocks or stones as you go. They don't need to be big — in fact, it's better if they're small enough that you can fit all of them in your pockets.

2. When you return home, wash and dry each of your rocks using water and paper towel.

3. Assign each rock a number, and create a column or special space on your notepaper for each of your rocks.

4. Measure the dimensions of each rock using your ruler or tape measure and describe each one's size in inches or millimeters.

5. Use your kitchen scale to determine the weight of each rock in ounces or grams. Mark each rock's weight down on your paper next to its size.

6. Working one rock at a time, use your magnifying glass to look closely at each one. Notice the different shapes, textures, colors, and finishes of the different rocks, and describe them in as much detail as possible on your notepaper.

7. Once you've cleaned, measured, weighed, and visually studied each of your 10 rocks, choose the three you find most interesting and use your reference materials (encyclopedia or internet) to try and see if you can learn what kind of rock or mineral it is. If you're using the internet, it can be useful to search what kinds of rock are most common in your area and compare your samples to pictures.

Follow-Up Questions:

1. What aspects or characteristics of the rocks you chose stood out to you? What did you notice during your up-close examination that impressed or surprised you?

_____

_____

2. Were you able to identify any of your rocks using online references? If so, what was one of them? If not, what made it hard for you to identify the rocks online?

_____

_____

YOGA

Please be aware of your environment and be safe at all times. If you cannot do an exercise, just try your best.

2 - Down Dog: 25 sec.

3 - Stretching: Stay as long as possible. Note: do on one leg then on another.

1 - Tree Pose: Stay as long as possible. Note: do on one leg then on another.

4 - Lower Plank: 12 sec. Note: Keep your back straight and body tight.

5 - Book Pose: 15 sec. Note: Keep your core tight. Legs should be across from your eyes.

6 - Shavasana: 5 min. Note: this pose is very important and provides you with long term benefits. Try not to skip this. Close your eyes and imagine who you want to be and what your goals are! Always think happy thoughts.

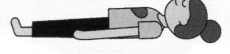

Task: Complete the jigsaw puzzle below. Which piece belongs to which letter?

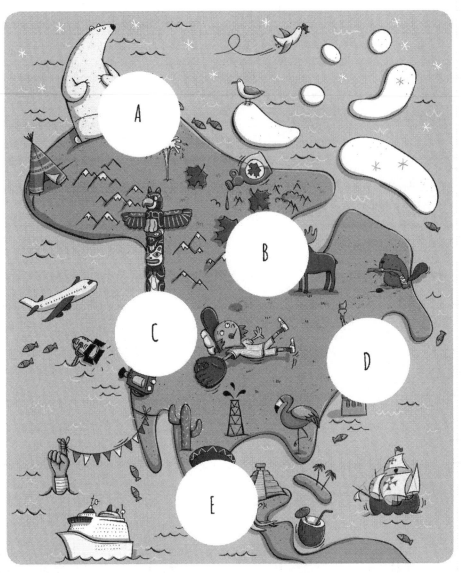

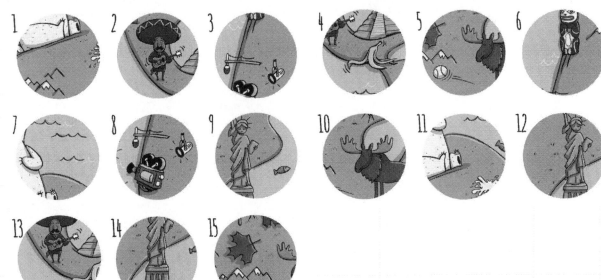

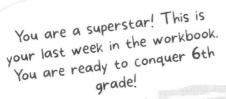

You are a superstar! This is your last week in the workbook. You are ready to conquer 6th grade!

WEEK 12

We are classified as Homo sapiens. Hundreds of thousands of years ago, early humans gathered and hunted for food. We have come very far and continue to advance as humans!

Fact vs. Opinion

More and more, being a good reader in today's world involves identifying and understanding the difference between **fact** and **opinion**. While fact and opinion are both valuable and important parts of our lives, mistaking an opinion for a fact can have catastrophic consequences. Part of the problem is that one of the ways that really good writers make their work convincing is by treating their opinions as though they were facts.

In order to double-check that you're accessing **facts**, it's important to study the claims a writer is making, the language they use to make those claims, and the evidence they use to support themselves.

Key Terms

Fact: Something that is indisputably <u>true</u> that can be <u>proven</u> with a great deal of evidence.

Opinion: The way a person or group of people think or feel about a particular issue.

Hints:

- Anytime someone says "I think" or "I believe" or mentions their own **personal perspective**, it's highly likely you're reading an **opinion.**

- Anytime someone is using **judgmental language** like "best," "worst," or "favorite" to rank or rate things, it's probably an **opinion.**

- If a **reasonable** person could disagree with something and provide an equally well-supported viewpoint, it's probably an opinion.

- If an author **can't provide any concrete evidence or support** for his or her idea, it is almost certainly an **opinion**

For Example...

- It is 70 degrees outside today.

  * This is a **simple statement of fact.**
  * Unless we have a thermometer and can prove that this statement is a lie, it's definitely a **fact!** You can't have an opinion about measurable things like what temperature it is!

- Ms. Pucksawl is the best teacher at our school.

  * This is an **opinion** – We know because another student could reasonably **disagree** without necessarily being wrong. For example, someone could say, "No way! Mr. Howard is the best teacher here!"

- Ms. Pucksawl is a popular teacher.

  * As long as at least half of students like Ms. Pucksawl, this is a **fact!**
  * "Popular" simply means "liked by more than half of people"
  * As you can see, this sentence is very close to the one before it, which was an opinion. That's why we have to read so closely!

From "The Strange Case of Dr. Jekyll & Mr. Hyde"

By Robert Louis Stevenson

"Where Utterson was liked, he was liked well. Hosts loved to detain the dry lawyer, when the light-hearted and loose-tongued had already their foot on the threshold; they liked to sit a while in his unobtrusive company, practising for solitude, sobering their minds in the man's rich silence after the expense and strain of gaiety. To this rule, Dr. Jekyll was no exception; and as he now sat on the opposite side of the fire—a large, well-made, smooth-faced man of fifty, with something of a stylish cast perhaps, but every mark of capacity and kindness—you could see by his looks that he cherished for Mr. Utterson a sincere and warm affection.

"I have been wanting to speak to you, Jekyll," began the latter. "You know that will of yours?"

A close observer might have gathered that the topic was distasteful; but the doctor carried it off lightly. "My poor Utterson," said he, "you are unfortunate in such a client. I never saw a man so distressed as you were by my will; unless it were that hide-bound pedant, Lanyon, at what he called my scientific heresies. O, I know he's a good fellow—you needn't frown—an excellent fellow, and I always mean to see more of him; but a hide-bound pedant for all that; an ignorant, blatant pedant. I was never more disappointed in any man than Lanyon."

"You know I never approved of it," pursued Utterson, ruthlessly disregarding the fresh topic.

"My will? Yes, certainly, I know that," said the doctor, a trifle sharply. "You have told me so."

"Well, I tell you so again," continued the lawyer. "I have been learning something of young Hyde."

The large handsome face of Dr. Jekyll grew pale to the very lips, and there came a blackness about his eyes. "I do not care to hear more," said he. "This is a matter I thought we had agreed to drop."

"What I heard was abominable," said Utterson.

"It can make no change. You do not understand my position," returned the doctor, with a certain incoherency of manner. "I am painfully situated, Utterson; my position is a very strange—a very strange one. It is one of those affairs that cannot be mended by talking."

"Jekyll," said Utterson, "you know me: I am a man to be trusted. It we can speak honestly in confidence, I make no doubt I can get you out of it."

"My good Utterson," said the doctor, "this is very good of you, this is downright good of you, and I cannot find words to thank you in. I believe you fully; I would trust you before any man alive, ay, before myself, if I could make the choice; but indeed it isn't what you fancy; it is not as bad as that; and just to put your good heart at rest, I will tell you[...]"

1. How would you describe **Dr. Jekyll's personality,** based on the passage?

   _____

   _____

2. How would you describe **Mr. Utterson's personality,** based on the passage?

   _____

   _____

3. Why does Mr. Utterson **stay** after Dr. Jekyll's other guests have left?

   A. Because they are best friends
   B. Because he is planning on sleeping at Dr. Jekyll's house that night
   C. Because he ate and drank too much and does not feel ready to leave
   D. Because he wants to have a private conversation with Dr. Jekyll

4. How would you describe Dr. Jekyll's answers when he is questioned about Mr. Hyde?

   A. Mysterious
   B. Angry
   C. Frustrated
   D. Light-hearted

5. In the chapter before this passage, Mr. Utterson learned that Dr. Jekyll has changed his will and left everything to Mr. Hyde. **Why** is that something that might be a cause for concern with Utterson?

   _____

   _____

   _____

   _____

   _____

   _____

Fact or Opinion?

Directions: Each sentence below represents either a statement of fact or an opinion. Read the sentences; then, on the lines below, indicate whether each sentence is based in **FACT** or **OPINION**. Once you've done that <u>circle the words from the sentence</u> that were hints to you.

1. That company makes the most beautiful watches on Earth.

   _____

2. The average temperature on the top of Mount Washington is 27 degrees Fahrenheit.

   _____

3. The Country Café is popular, but nobody likes the pancakes there.

   _____

4. Statistics show that mid-sized sedans are the most popular cars in America.

   _____

5. When it comes to basketball players, scoring is more important than the ability to play defense or rebound.

   _____

FITNESS

Please be aware of your environment and be safe at all times. If you cannot do an exercise, just try your best.

Repeat these exercises 4 ROUNDS

1 - Abs: 15 times

2 - Lunges: 4 times to each leg.
Note: Use your body weight or books as weight to do leg lunges.

4 - Run: 50m
Note: Run 25 meters to one side and 25 meters back to the starting position.

3 - Plank: 20 sec.

From "The Strange Case of Dr. Jekyll & Mr. Hyde"

By Robert Louis Stevenson

Nearly a year later, in the month of October, 18—, London was startled by a crime of singular ferocity and rendered all the more notable by the high position of the victim. The details were few and startling. A maid servant living alone in a house not far from the river, had gone upstairs to bed about eleven. Although a fog rolled over the city in the small hours, the early part of the night was cloudless, and the lane, which the maid's window overlooked, was brilliantly lit by the full moon. It seems she was romantically given, for she sat down upon her box, which stood immediately under the window, and fell into a dream of musing.

Never (she used to say, with streaming tears, when she narrated that experience), never had she felt more at peace with all men or thought more kindly of the world. And as she so sat she became aware of an aged beautiful gentleman with white hair, drawing near along the lane; and advancing to meet him, another and very small gentleman, to whom at first she paid less attention. When they had come within speech (which was just under the maid's eyes) the older man bowed and accosted the other with a very pretty manner of politeness.

It did not seem as if the subject of his address were of great importance; indeed, from his pointing, it some times appeared as if he were only inquiring his way; but the moon shone on his face as he spoke, and the girl was pleased to watch it, it seemed to breathe such an innocent and old-world kindness of disposition, yet with something high too, as of a well-founded self-content. Presently her eye wandered to the other, and she was surprised to recognise in him a certain Mr. Hyde, who had once visited her master and for whom she had conceived a dislike.

He had in his hand a heavy cane, with which he was trifling; but he answered never a word, and seemed to listen with an ill-contained impatience. And then all of a sudden he broke out in a great flame of anger, stamping with his foot, brandishing the cane, and carrying on (as the maid described it) like a madman. The old gentleman took a step back, with the air of one very much surprised and a trifle hurt; and at that Mr. Hyde broke out of all bounds and clubbed him to the earth. And next moment, with ape-like fury, he was trampling his victim under foot and hailing down a storm of blows. At the horror of these sights and sounds, the maid fainted.

1. How do the tone and feeling of the first paragraph and a half differ from the second half of the passage?

_____

_____

2. How does Mr. Hyde's personality seem to the maid before he attacks the old man?

_____

_____

3. Which character does the maid describe as though they were almost perfect?

   A. Herself
   B. The old man
   C. Dr. Jekyll
   D. Mr. Utterson

4. What is most shocking to the maid?

   A. That Mr. Hyde gets violently angry, seemingly out of nowhere
   B. That the old man is walking by himself late at night
   C. That Mr. Hyde turns into an ape
   D. That the old man is polite, even to someone as ugly as Mr. Hyde

5. How does the content of this passage connect to Dr. Utterson's earlier concerns in Day One's passage?

_____

_____

_____

_____

_____

Fact or Opinion? Part 2

Directions: Each sentence below represents either a statement of fact or an opinion. Read the sentences; then, on the lines below, indicate whether each sentence is based in **FACT** or **OPINION**. Once you've done that <u>circle the words from the sentence</u> that were hints to you.

1. Our office provides competitive healthcare benefit packages to all employees.

_____

2. Our company is a great place to work because everybody here thinks of the team as a big family.

_____

3. Tennis is not as exciting to watch as other sports because you have to focus on the same two players for a long time.

_____

4. Most people live with electricity because, given the conveniences people are used to today, life would be extremely difficult without it.

_____

5. Lemons are the perfect fruit to use in dessert because their acidity helps your stomach fight the richness of the food you just ate.

_____

FITNESS

Please be aware of your environment and be safe at all times. If you cannot do an exercise, just try your best.

Repeat these **exercises** **4 ROUNDS**

1 - Squats: 15 times. Note: imagine you are trying to sit on a chair.

2 - Side Bending: 10 times to each side. Note: try to touch your feet.

3 - Tree Pose: Stay as long as possible. Note: do the same with the other leg.

End of Summer Assessment (Mixed Questions):

1. There are 864 stickers and Amanda uses 352 stickers while grading student's homework papers. How many stickers are left?

2. Steven bought three pairs of socks and two T-shirts. One pair of socks cost $2.55 and one T-shirt cost $15.50. How much did Steven spend on clothes in total?

The model below shows how many cookies Christina ate. Use the model to solve problems **3 - 5**.

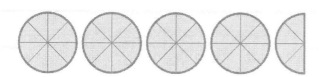

3. If Henry ate $3\frac{3}{8}$ as many cookies as Christina, how many cookies did Henry eat?

4. Jesse ate $5\frac{6}{8}$ as many cookies as Christina. How many cookies did Jesse eat?

5. Mike ate double what Chistina ate. How many cookies did Mike eat?

6. What is the product of $\frac{9}{21} \times \frac{1}{3}$?

7. Which number would complete the equation: $\frac{?}{8} \times \frac{5}{9} = \frac{35}{72}$

8. The shaded part of the square below has a length of $\frac{7}{8}$ cm and the width of $\frac{3}{4}$ cm.

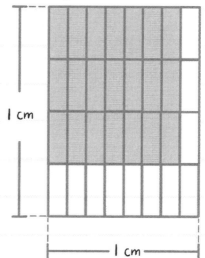

1 cm

1 cm

What is the area of the shaded part of the square in square cm?

A. $\frac{3}{8}$ sq cm   C. $\frac{10}{12}$ sq cm

B. $\frac{7}{4}$ sq cm   D. $\frac{21}{32}$ sq cm

9. What is $\frac{4}{14} + \frac{2}{5}$?

A. $\frac{6}{19}$

B. $\frac{22}{70}$

C. $\frac{24}{35}$

D. $\frac{24}{70}$

10. Solve the problem $\frac{3}{5} - \frac{4}{16}$.

A. $\frac{1}{4}$ C. $\frac{1}{20}$

B. $\frac{7}{20}$ D. $\frac{1}{11}$

11. Find a fraction that makes the number sentence true.

$$\frac{4}{9} > \underline{\hspace{2cm}}$$

A. $\frac{12}{25}$ C. $\frac{9}{16}$

B. $\frac{6}{10}$ D. $\frac{12}{32}$

12. Order the following fractions from least to greatest $\frac{8}{12}, \frac{11}{20}, \frac{5}{6}, \frac{3}{15}$.

13. What is $\frac{4}{8} + \frac{15}{24}$?

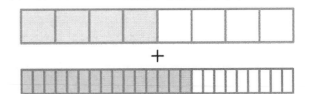

14. The product of $\frac{6}{18} \times 3$ is:

A. Less than 1

B. Equal to 1

C. Greater than 1

D. None of the above

15. What is $7\frac{2}{8} \times 5$?

A. $7\frac{10}{40}$ C. $35\frac{10}{40}$

B. $8\frac{2}{8}$ D. $36\frac{1}{4}$

FITNESS

Please be aware of your environment and be safe at all times. If you cannot do an exercise, just try your best.

Repeat these **exercises 4 ROUNDS**

2 - Lunges: 7 times to each leg.
Note: Use your body weight or books as weight to do leg lunges.

1 - Bend forward: 15 times.
Note: try to touch your feet. Make sure to keep your back straight and if needed you can bend your knees.

4 - Abs: 15 times

3 - Plank: 20 sec.

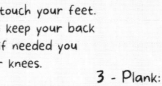

End of Summer Assessment (Mixed Questions):

1. The perimeter of the rectangle is 44 inches. What is the area of the shaded part?

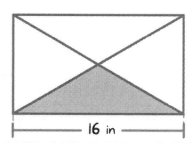

16 in

2. Which of the following expressions best represents: find K times as much as 8?

A. 8 - K   C. 8 ÷ K
B. 8 × K   D. K ÷ 8

3. What is the value of the expression $a^2 - 4(b + 3)$, if $a = 8$ and $b = 12$?

4. The height of a ladder is 168 inches. What is the height of the ladder in feet?

5. What is the volume of the rectangular prism?

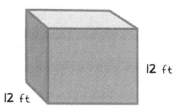

12 ft
12 ft
24 ft

6. Draw all lines of symmetry for this shape.

7. Grandma Lucy measured her grandchildren's yearly growth. The results are shown below.

Grandchildren's yearly growth

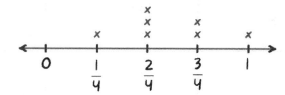

How many grandchildren does grandmam Lucy have?

Use the graph below to answer questions 8 - 9.

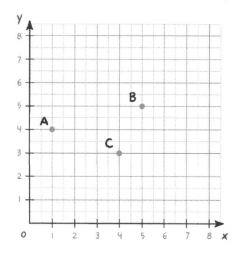

8. What are the coordinates for Point C?

A. (3, 4)   C. (5, 5)
B. (4, 3)   D. (4, 6)

9. Which point is located at (1, 4)?

   A. A

   B. B

   C. C

   D. D

10. Which statement is true?

   A. All parallelograms have four sides of equal length.

   B. All parallelograms are squares.

   C. All parallelograms are rhombuses.

   D. All parallelograms are quadrilaterals.

11. Is this shape a quadrilateral?

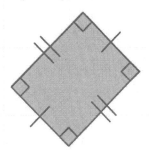

12. What is the solution to this equation: $\frac{48}{x} = 6$?

   A. $x = 6$ C. $x = 8$

   B. $x = 7$ D. $x = 9$

13. Solve the problem $z - 124 = 372$.

   A. $z = 346$ C. $z = 456$

   B. $z = 396$ D. $z = 496$

14. Find the area of this triangle.

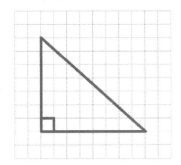

   A. 56 square units

   B. 49 square units

   C. 32 square units

   D. 28 square units

FITNESS

Please be aware of your environment and be safe at all times. If you cannot do an exercise, just try your best.

Repeat these **exercises 4 ROUNDS**

1 - High Plank: 20 sec.

2 - Chair: 15 sec. Note: sit on an imaginary chair, keep your back straight.

3 - Waist Hooping: 15 times. Note: if you do not have a hoop, pretend you have an imaginary hoop and rotate your hips 10 times.

4 - Abs: 15 times

End of Summer Assessment (Mixed Questions):

1. Determine the greatest common factor of 24 and 48.

   A. 24   C. 6

   B. 12   D. 4

2. What is another way to express 46 − 28?

_____

3. Add 684,932 to 345,179.

_____

4. Which number should be added to 139,575 to get the number 637,911?

   A. 449,726

   B. 498,336

   C. 512,916

   D. 522,766

5. Choose an option in which there is an expression to get 317,516.

   A. 562,127 − 244,611

   B. 675,933 − 342,567

   C. 428,916 − 110,410

   D. 539,177 − 221,321

6. What is the missing number in this equation 56,128 − _____ = 22,149?

_____

7. What is the missing number in the equation _____ × 72 = 11,448?

   A. 129   C. 149

   B. 139   D. 159

8. Choose the right multiplier for 975 to get 26,325.

   A. 25   C. 35

   B. 27   D. 37

9. Find the divider of 936 to get 72.

   A. 13   C. 17

   B. 15   D. 19

10. What is 3,484 ÷ 26?

   A. 114   C. 134

   B. 124   D. 144

11. Divide 96 by 3, using the models below.

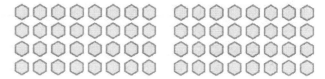

_____

12. Which digit represents the hundredths place in the number 7,849.156?

_____

13. In the number 873.168 the digit 7 is in what place value?

   A. Hundreds

   B. Tens

   C. Tenths

   D. Hundredths

14. Which combination of numbers is the expanded form of 9,506,349?

   A. 500,000 + 9 + 300 + 60,000 + 9,000,000 + 40

   B. 40 + 900,000 + 6,000 + 50,000 + 9 + 300

   C. 500,000 + 300 + 9,000,000 + 40 + 6,000 + 9

   D. 300 + 9,000,000 + 9 + 6,000 + 50,000 + 40

15. What is 30 + 40,000 + 700 + 2 + 300,000 + 5,000 + 4,000,000 in standard form?

   A. 3,454,732

   B. 3,547,432

   C. 4,354,732

   D. 4,345,732

16. Solve the problem $(135 + 268) \times 5$.

   A. 1,985   C. 2,095

   B. 2,015   D. 2,135

17. Calculate $(23 - 14) \times (345 + 296)$.

18. Which rule describes the pattern 3, 18, 108, 648 ...?

   A. Add 15   C. Times 6

   B. Add 90   D. Times 12

19. What is the missing number in this pattern 4, 11, 20, 31, ..., 59, 76?

20. Fill in the missing cells in the table below.

Input (x)	6	8		32	57	63
Output (y)	21	23	29	47		78

YOGA

Please be aware of your environment and be safe at all times. If you cannot do an exercise, just try your best.

1 - Down Dog: 25 sec.

2 - Bend Down: 25 sec.

3 - Chair: 20 sec.

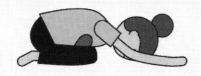

5 - Shavasana: as long as you can. Note: think of happy moments and relax your mind.

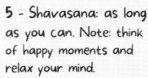

EXPERIMENT

The Greenhouse Effect

There's a great deal of misunderstanding about how man-made pollution can lead to climate change. Excess waste gases like carbon dioxide and methane get trapped within our planet's atmosphere, acting like a blanket that traps heat down closer to the Earth. We call this process **the greenhouse effect**. Today, we'll do a quick experiment to help show how a layer of trapped gas can impact temperature.

Materials:

* 2 clean, dry mason jars or other sealable glass containers
* Cold running water
* A tray of ice cubes
* A clear plastic bag (like a freezer bag)
* A thermometer
* A timer
* Notepaper

Procedure:

1. Fill each of your two jars with two cups of the coldest possible water you can get out of your sink.

2. Add 4-6 ice cubes to both jars. Make sure you add the same number to each one.

3. Place your thermometer in each jar to take its temperature. Mark the starting temperatures of both jars on your notepaper.

4. Place one of the two jars inside of the clear plastic bag.

5. On your notepaper, write a quick prediction about which jar you think will warm at a faster rate.

6. Look for a sunny place outdoors, like the middle of a driveway or yard, and place both jars right next to each other, one by itself and one in the plastic bag.

7. Set your timer for one hour.

8. When the timer goes off, go retrieve your jars and remove the one from its plastic bag.

9. Using your thermometer, check each jar's temperature again and record it on your notepaper.

10. Review your prediction from Step 5 and see if you were right. If you were right, what helped you understand what would happen ahead of time? If you were wrong, why did you think the way you did before the experiment?

Follow-Up Questions:

1. How did the plastic bag act like the trapped gasses of **the greenhouse effect?**

_____

_____

_____

2. Based on what you saw, why is the greenhouse effect potentially dangerous?

_____

_____

_____

YOGA

Please be aware of your environment and be safe at all times. If you cannot do an exercise, just try your best.

1 - Tree Pose: Stay as long as possible. Note: do on one leg then on another.

2 - Down Dog: 25 sec.

3 - Stretching: Stay as long as possible. Note: do on one leg then on another.

5 -Book Pose: 15 sec. Note: Keep your core tight. Legs should be across from your eyes.

4 - Lower Plank: 12 sec. Note: Keep your back straight and body tight.

6 - Shavasana: 5 min. Note: this pose is very important and provides you with long term benefits. Try not to skip this. Close your eyes and imagine who you want to be and what your goals are! Always think happy thoughts.

Task: There are four different umbrellas shown. There is a top view and a side view for each of the umbrellas. Pair up the identical umbrellas.

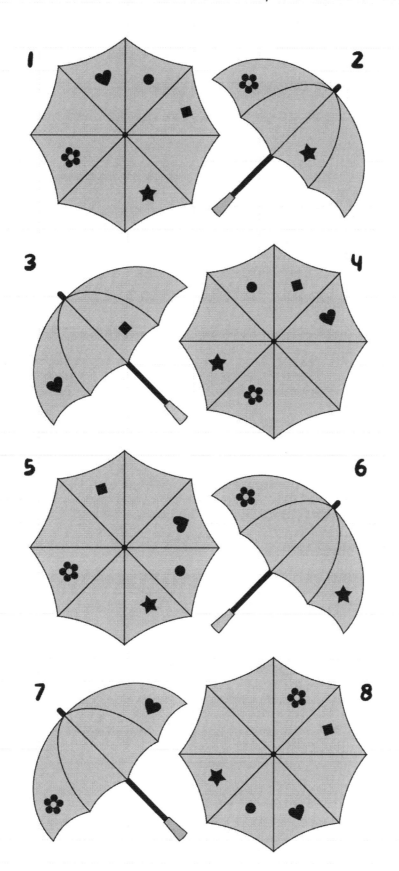

ANSWER SHEET

WEEK 1 🦕 DAY 1

READING COMPREHENSION:

1. Said is an action verb. The reader should be able to identify it as such because "saying" something is an action that can easily be visualized. Also, it cannot be a linking verb because it would alter the meaning of the sentence to replace "said" with a form of "to be" and say, "'Not long ago,' was he at length."

2. The author puts "little cliff" in quotation marks because he is being sarcastic. Based on Paragraph 3, the cliff is tall and narrow, and there's about a 1,500 foot drop-off if anybody were to fall.

3. B – The narrator can't shake the feeling that the cliffs are going to crumble out from beneath him. In Paragraph 3, the narrator says he "struggled in vain to divest [himself] of the idea that the very foundations of the mountain were in danger."

4. C – The passage could be described as ominous because the narrator keeps expressing the overwhelming feeling that something bad is going to happen, and the cliff they are exploring seems incredibly dangerous.

5. Answers will slightly vary. Students should be able to identify that the old man is confident and somewhat nonchalant about the cliff, while the narrator is completely terrified and worried. Based on the final paragraph, we know that the old man is very detail-oriented and fact-based, while the narrator seems to let his anxiety and imagination get away from him.

ENGLISH/GRAMMAR ACTIVITY:

1. Linking   2. Action   3. Linking   4. Action   5. Linking

WEEK 1 🦕 DAY 1

READING COMPREHENSION:

1. Answers will vary. In Paragraph 1, the author describes the creepy sound that the maelstrom makes as being like the moaning of buffaloes. The wind is described as having "monstrous velocity." The sea itself is described as having "ungovernable fury." In the final sentences of Paragraph 2, the author also describes the horrifying sound in great detail.

2. The reader can observe things escalating when the dull moaning and nasty winds of the first paragraph seem to subside momentarily before evolving into the terrifying maelstrom of Paragraph 2.

3. C – The description of the herd of buffalo is used to describe the noise of the sea in Paragraph 1. Earlier in the sentence that contains the word "buffalo," the author writes, "I became aware of a loud and gradually increasing sound."

ANSWER SHEET

4. B – Paragraph **2** describes a series of small whirlpools growing into one gigantic one. The description of the "mouth of the terrific funnel" should have been a major indicator to the reader.

5. Answers will vary. Water is described as being terrifying and destructive in the passage. It makes loud, unnerving sounds and gets whipped up into incredibly huge and destructive whirlpools.

ENGLISH/GRAMMAR ACTIVITY:

1. The verb in the sentence is "talked," and it is an action verb.

2. The first verb in the sentence is "appears," which is a linking verb. The second verb in the sentence is "is," which is a linking verb.

3. The verb in the sentence is "traveled," and it is an action verb.

4. The verb in the sentence is "learn," and it is an action verb.

5. The first verb in the sentence is "look," and it is a linking verb. The second verb in the sentence is "rely," and it is an action verb.

WEEK 1 DAY 3

Addition Problems

1. B
2. C
3. D
4. B
5. A
6. B
7. C
8. 71,483
9. 56,784 + 46,842 = 103,626
10. B
11. 71,828
12. 12,431

13. D
14. C
15. C
16. B
17. C
18. B
19. C
20. 43,837

WEEK 1 DAY 4

Subtraction Problems

1. C
2. A
3. D
4. C
5. D

6. False - 51,564
7. 22,836
8. 234,367
9. 14,492
10. 28,042
11. C
12. B
13. D
14. C
15. C
16. B
17. A
18. C
19. B
20. C

ANSWER SHEET

WEEK 1 ✦ DAY 5

Multiplication Problems

1. A
2. B
3. A
4. C
5. B

6. 73,450
7. A
8. 244,800
9. 116,512
10. C
11. C
12. B
13. D

14. A
15. C
16. B
17. A
18. 45,625
19. 261,688
20. 483,700

WEEK 1 ✦ DAY 6

Answers will vary.

WEEK 2 ✦ DAY 1

READING COMPREHENSION:

1. The author is acknowledging that his definition of "fossil" seems very general and non-specific. The sentences that follow in Paragraph 1 explain that defining the term "fossil" is so difficult because there are many different objects that can be considered "fossils."

2. Generally, fossil finds are either imprints like footprints or bones that have turned to stone. However, in Paragraph 2, the author explains that some wooly mammoths have been found frozen in ice with skin, hair, and tissue remaining.

3. D – In the opening sentences of Paragraph 2, the author establishes that bones of the Great Auk and Rytina would not be considered fossils, even though they are extinct. This shows that their remains are not old enough to have fossilized and turn to stone, which suggests they became extinct shortly before the passage was written.

4. B – This passage is written for a general audience who is trying to gain basic information about fossils. There is no highly-technical language that suggests it is for an audience of experts, and there are no tips that suggest it is meant as an instructional piece for people hoping to find fossils.

5. Answers will vary somewhat. There are many different kinds of remains that can be classified as fossils. For example, a fossil could be a bone that has turned into stone, or a fossil could be a footprint that has been preserved over millions of years. Additionally, fossils don't just come from animals. Plants, insects, and other organisms can create fossil remains as well.

ANSWER SHEET

ENGLISH/GRAMMAR ACTIVITY:

1. The line should be drawn after "fox"

2. The line should be drawn after "great-uncle"

3. The line should be drawn after "Samantha"

4. The line should be drawn after "scientist"

5. The line should be drawn after "band"

WEEK 2 DAY 2

READING COMPREHENSION:

1. The author mentions dogs (specifically hyenas) and mice to illustrate why not many remains actually turn into fossils. Dogs like hyenas take and eat bones, while mice damage remains by gnawing on them or burrowing through them.

2. In Paragraph 2, the author discusses how the roots of plants can grow and spread through bones and other remains in a way that breaks them apart and destroys them, "like so many little wedges."

3. B – "The work of the elements" is the subject of the sentence, and "is aided" is the main verb. Therefore, the sentence should be divided directly between the subject and the verb.

4. C – The third paragraph of the passage explains that, while deserts and oceans are bad places for fossil preservation, lakes, streams, and rivers are some of the best places for remains to be preserved.

5. The passage explains that not every bone can become a fossil due to a variety of natural processes. Scavenging predators and other animals frequently pick or steal remains as food, and the roots of growing plants can destroy bones buried underground. Only very specific conditions (like the thick mud of a riverbed) and some degree of luck lead to a bone becoming a fossil.

ENGLISH/GRAMMAR ACTIVITY:

1. Correct.

2. Incorrect. "The legendary comedy duo of Abbott and Costello" is the complete subject, and "made more than 35 movies together" is the complete predicate.

3. Incorrect. "Sylvia and Becky" is the complete subject, and "always eat lunch on the steps of the library" is the predicate.

4. Incorrect. "All of the king's horses and all the king's men" is the complete subject, and "couldn't put Humpty Dumpty together again" is the complete predicate.

5. Incorrect. "Some people" is the complete subject, and "believe paying taxes is actually a privilege" is the complete predicate.

ANSWER SHEET

WEEK 2 DAY 3

Word problems: add/subtract/multiply/divide

1. 1,288
2. C
3. B
4. A
5. 101,700
6. 25,763
7. D
8. B
9. C
10. 570
11. 97,536
12. B
13. 97
14. 42
15. 120 minutes or 2 hours
16. 296
17. 411

WEEK 2 DAY 4

Diagrams: add/subtract/multiply/divide

1. 1,312
2. 25,732 + 12,434 = 38,166
3. B
4. C
5. 16 × 14 = 224
6. 6
7. 25,348 − 12,162 = 13,186

WEEK 2 DAY 5

Place Value

1. B
2. C
3. A
4. B
5. A
6. D

7. C
8. 2,381,547
9. one thousand
10. 1
11. 3.658
12. B
13. B
14. 8
15. D
16. A
17. B

WEEK 2 DAY 7

Answers will vary.

WEEK 3 DAY 1

READING COMPREHENSION:

1. Based on the passage, the Celts, Romans, Goths, Burgundians, Jura, Franks, and Teutons all lived in the area we now call France at various times.

2. Rome controlled various parts of France (which they called Gaul) in ancient times, and many of the Gauls and Franks adopted Roman religion, language, and culture.

3. C – The opening sentence of Paragraph 2 identifies that the Celts were the earliest recorded inhabitants of France. All the other answer choices are presented as having happened later in history.

4. D – Paragraph 1 provides a short geographic description of what constitutes France. It includes water features and mountain ranges that help the reader understand where France is located and what kind of geographical features it contains.

5. When the author says France became France "by degrees," she means that it was a gradual process that took a long time. The passage shows that the French border and cultural identity was created over thousands of years of interactions between Celts, Romans, Franks, and others.

ENGLISH/GRAMMAR ACTIVITY:

1. "All cows" is the complete subject. "Cows" is the simple subject. "Eat grass" is the complete predicate. "Eat" is the simple predicate.

2. "George Washington and his troops" is the complete subject. "George Washington" and "troops" are the simple subjects. "Camped in Valley Forge for about six months in 1777 and 1778" is the complete predicate. "Camped" is the simple predicate.

3. "My sister Malory" is the complete subject. "Malory" is the simple subject. "Learned to type using online software" is the complete predicate. "Learned" is the simple predicate.

4. "The biggest and most impressive carnival we went to last summer" is the complete subject. "Carnival" is the simple subject. "Was at the state fair" is the complete predicate. "Was" is the simple predicate.

5. "The long caravan of weekend cyclists" is the complete subject. "Caravan" is the simple subject. "Caused major problems for everybody driving down the scenic highway" is the complete predicate. "Caused" is the simple predicate.

WEEK 3 DAY 2

READING COMPREHENSION:

1. Defending Paris from the Northmen (Danes) was an important cause that brought the various Frankish leaders together in unity. Paragraph 3 shows that this shared cause was a major factor in the formation of France, as we know it.

2. The Northmen, who were also known as the Danes, were pirate-like invaders who attacked coastal areas in Europe. Many of the Frankish leaders banded together to fight the Northmen, which brought the area together in a way that led to creating a unified kingdom, which ultimately became France.

3. B – Paragraph 1 establishes that "Danes" and "Northmen" are synonyms for each other. The first sentence of Paragraph 2 establishes that the Northmen/Danes were "pirates."

4. C – "All the after kings of France down to Louis Philippe" is the complete subject of the sentence. "Were descendants of Hugh Capet" is the complete predicate. "Kings" is the simple subject and "were" is the simple predicate.

ANSWER SHEET

5. Based on Paragraph 3, even though Hugh Capet was regarded as the king of all the Franks, he only really controlled the areas immediately around Paris. In other parts of the country, local leaders still ruled however they wanted.

ENGLISH/GRAMMAR ACTIVITY:

1. "Tonya's beautiful wedding gown" is the complete subject. "Gown" is the simple subject. "Sparkled in the sunlight as she walked down the aisle" is the complete predicate. "Sparkled" is the simple predicate.

2. "Mikael, our foreign exchange student" is the complete subject. "Mikael" is the simple subject. "Has an impressive collection of rocks and geodes from around the world" is the complete predicate. "Has" is the simple predicate.

3. "The idea that all rivers flow south" is the complete subject. "Idea" is the simple subject. "Is a major misconception among students" is the complete predicate. "Is" is the simple predicate.

4. "Hands-on projects" is the complete subject. "Projects" is the simple subject. "Provide young learners with opportunities to demonstrate what they know and what they're capable of" is the complete predicate. "Provide" is the simple predicate.

5. "The family of inexperienced campers" is the complete subject. "Family" is the simple subject. "accidentally started a small forest fire when they didn't dispose of ashes properly" is the complete predicate. "Started" is the simple predicate.

WEEK 3 · DAY 3

Evaluating Expessions

1. D
2. B
3. C
4. 6,804
5. 35
6. 125
7.
    A. 32,292
    B. 14
    C. 1,280
    D. 3,422
8. B
9. C
10. D
11. 509,175
12. A
13.
    * 197
    * 3,780
14. 16,375
15. 254
16. 6
17. 28,490
18. 328
19. 56
20. 5,174

WEEK 3 · DAY 4

Patterns

1. B
2. D
3. C
4. 3, 15, 75, 375, **1,875**
5. A
6. 12, 48, 192, **768,** 3,072
7. B
8. $x - 12 = y$
9. D
10. $k \times 4 = m$

226

ANSWER SHEET

11.

Input (x)	2	6	7	9	15	22
Output (y)	13	17	18	20	26	**33**

12.

Input (x)	12	39	**48**	72	99	**129**
Output (y)	4	13	16	**24**	33	43

13.

x	2	4	6	8
y	3	4	5	6

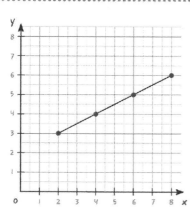

WEEK 3 DAY 5

Comparing numbers and decimals

1. $8,976,235 < 8,976,251$

2. D

3. C

4.
   A. $5.672 < 5.677$
   B. $46.872 > 4.978$
   C. $0.187 > 0.065$
   D. $56.709 < 476.98$

5. B

WEEK 3 DAY 6

Answers will vary.

6. B

7.
   A. $11,014 > 10,930$
   B. $2,820 < 5,024$
   C. $1,242 > 858$
   D. $1,894 < 2,827$

8. B

9. $56.932 > 56.8765$

10. $6.732, 6.954, 59.347, 65.43$

11.
   A. $56 < 56.128$
   B. $472 > 47.289$
   C. $8,934.278 < 8,934,209$
   D. $7.008 < 7.100$

12. $134.27, 46.01, 24.956, 3.803, 3.781$

13. D

14.
   A. $1,600 > 1,564$
   B. $375 > 234$
   C. $904 < 954$
   D. $1,376 > 1,012$

15. $782 < 812$

16. C

17.
   A. $4.932 < 5.068$
   B. $34.76 > 3.489$
   C. $12.956 < 1,134.9$
   D. $6.096 < 6.132$

18. B

ANSWER SHEET

WEEK 4 ● DAY 1

READING COMPREHENSION:

1. Based on the title and formatting of the passage, the reader can infer that this comes from a book that contains explanations and descriptions of many different trees, including information about what the trees are called, how to identify them, and where they grow.

2. According to the final paragraph of the passage, you must study the trees' shapes to classify them in the winter. Larches are broader and more cone-shaped, whereas the cypress is skinnier and taller.

3. A - This passage is mostly focused on helping the reader identify these trees and tell them apart from each other. The subheadings ("How to tell them from other trees" and "How to tell them from each other") should be major indicators to the reader.

4. B - Paragraph 2 provides a list of different locations where larches and cypresses can be found. While the paragraph hints at the various different species of larch and cypress, it does not identify or explain any of them.

5. Answers will vary. Students should identify that the two trees are largely similar in appearance and, unlike other conifers, both drop their leaves in the fall.

ENGLISH/GRAMMAR ACTIVITY:

1. "And" - Coordinating

2. "Because" - Subordinating; "Neither... nor" - Correlative

3. "Even though" - Subordinating

4. "Since" - Subordinating

5. "As" - Subordinating

WEEK 4 ● DAY 2

READING COMPREHENSION:

1. According to Paragraph 3, white oaks grow new batches of acorns each year. That means, all the acorns on a tree at any given time grew in the same year. On the other hand, black oaks have two different batches of acorns on them: new acorns from this year and maturing acorns from last year.

2. Answers will vary. Generally, the description of the bark helps students understand the color and texture of the outside of the tree. The shapes of the buds, leaves, and acorns also provide valuable details for the reader.

ANSWER SHEET

3. D – Under "Range," the passage clearly identifies that white oaks are primarily found in Eastern North America. Los Angeles is on the west coast of North America, so it is the only choice that does not align with the described range.

4. C – "And" is one of the basic coordinating conjunctions. None of the other options are conjunctions.

5. Answers will vary. Students might suggest that the inclusion of pictures would be useful.

ENGLISH/GRAMMAR ACTIVITY:

1. Nor
2. Even though
3. Not only
4. As
5. But

WEEK 4 DAY 3

Word problems: add/subtract for fractions

1. $10\frac{1}{4}$ kg
2. $9\frac{7}{12}$ feet
3. $\frac{17}{40}$ of a mile
4. $\frac{7}{45}$ glasses
5. $\frac{13}{20}$
6. $\frac{10}{12}$ or $\frac{5}{6}$ kg
7. $\frac{1}{25}$ mile
8. $13\frac{55}{72}$ pages/hour
9. $\frac{39}{40}$ hours
10. $\frac{27}{20}$ or $1\frac{7}{20}$ lbs
11. $\frac{11}{60}$ cups
12. C

13. 6
14. $3\frac{28}{30}$ or $3\frac{14}{15}$ hours
15. $\frac{2}{4}$ or $\frac{1}{2}$ cups

WEEK 4 DAY 4

Comparing fractions

1. D
2. B
3. C
4. A
5. B
6. D
7. C
8. D
9. B
10. A
11. $\frac{4}{9} > \frac{3}{8}$
12. $\frac{16}{20} > \frac{24}{36}$
13. $\frac{2}{7} = \frac{14}{49}$
14. $\frac{6}{14} < \frac{9}{20}$
15. $\frac{13}{39} = \frac{25}{75}$

WEEK 4 DAY 5

Shading in fraction models

1. C
2. $\frac{14}{40}$
3. D
4. $\frac{21}{18}$ or $1\frac{1}{6}$
5. B
6. $7\frac{6}{8}$
7. C
8. D
9. $\frac{64}{60}$ or $1\frac{4}{60}$
10. $\frac{8}{45}$

WEEK 4 DAY 6

Answers will vary.

229

ANSWER SHEET

WEEK 5 • DAY 1

READING COMPREHENSION:

1. Jack believes that the country is "excessively boring" because there is nothing to do. He also expresses that he strongly dislikes his neighbors in the country.

2. Jack realizes that Algernon must be receiving guests when he sees the cucumber sandwiches and the large number of cups on the table. The excessive amount of food and drinks leads him to infer that more people are arriving.

3. A - This passage contains a great deal of humor. Jack's descriptions of boring country life, his vocal distaste for his neighbors, and way of speaking ("How perfectly delightful!") are all humorous. Algernon seems to be sarcastic and funny as well, based on his joke that proclaiming one's love for someone else is "business" rather than pleasure.

4. C - We know Jack is a romantic because of his incredible love for Gwendolen and his insistence on proposing to her. On the other hand, Algernon seems dismissive of love and sarcastically says that Jack coming to town to propose is basically a business trip.

5. Answers will vary. Students will probably predict that Jack and Gwendolen's romance will play out. Students may also predict that the cucumber sandwiches will be eaten. Students may predict there will be some kind of a conflict between Jack and Aunt Augusta, based on her disapproval.

ENGLISH/GRAMMAR ACTIVITY:

1. A comma should be inserted after "sweets" (to separate the intro from the body of the sentence).

2. A comma should be inserted after "business" (to separate the intro from the body of the sentence).

3. A comma should be inserted after "quietly" (to separate the intro from the body of the sentence).

4. Commas should be inserted after "Phil," "Bret," and (optionally) "Mike" (to separate the items in a list.

5. A comma should be inserted after "jump" (to create a compound sentence).

ANSWER SHEET

WEEK 5 DAY 2

READING COMPREHENSION:

1. Lady Bracknell is suggesting that Algernon enjoys misbehaving and doing silly, frivolous, or inappropriate things. She asks if he is "behaving" very well, meaning that she wonders if he is acting as he should. He responds that he is "feeling" very well, meaning that he is having fun and enjoying life.

2. Answers will vary. Lady Bracknell is very disapproving (both of Algernon's lifestyle and Jack's romance with Gwendolen), and she seems to enjoy telling other characters what they should do and how they should live. Based on her dismissal of Algernon, Jack, and Lady Harbury's husband, the reader can infer that Lady Bracknell generally disapproves of male behavior.

3. D - When Lady Bracknell says Lady Harbury "looks quite twenty years younger," she is suggesting that Lady Harbury actually looks better and happier now that her husband is dead. The implication is that Lady Harbury did not love or enjoy life with her husband.

4. C - "I'm sorry if we are a little late, Algernon" is one complete sentence. "I was obliged to call on dear Lady Harbury" is another complete sentence. The comma and conjunction "but" connect them into a compound sentence.

5. Based on the two passages, we know that Algernon (and his butler Lane) are lying when they say that there were no cucumbers. In Day One's passage, Jack specifically noticed the cucumber sandwiches on the table. It appears that all the sandwiches were eaten by Jack and Algernon before Lady Bracknell and Gwendolen arrived late.

ENGLISH/GRAMMAR ACTIVITY:

1. The comma after "and" should be circled.

2. The comma after "it" should be circled.

3. The comma after "disoriented" should be circled.

4. The comma after "decide" should be circled.

5. The comma after "even" should be circled.

ANSWER SHEET

WEEK 5 DAY 3

Interpreting fraction products

1. C
2. B
3. D
4. B
5. A
6. C
7. D
8. A
9. C
10. D
11. $\frac{50}{96}$
12. $10\frac{6}{8}$
13. $\frac{48}{15}$ or $3\frac{3}{15}$ or, $3\frac{1}{5}$

WEEK 5 DAY 4

Finding the area of a rectangle with fractional side lengths

1. A
2. C
3. B
4. A
5. D
6. B
7. D
8. C
9. B

WEEK 5 DAY 5

Problems with fractions and multiplication

1. B
2. C

3. D
4. C
5. B
6. B
7. D
8. A
9. A
10. C
11. D
12. A
13. $21\frac{4}{8}$ or $21\frac{1}{2}$
14. $\frac{10}{6}$ or $1\frac{4}{6}$ or $1\frac{2}{3}$
15. 5
16. $\frac{18}{14} > 1$
17. 6
18. $31\frac{5}{20}$ or $31\frac{1}{4}$

WEEK 5 DAY 6

Answers will vary.

WEEK 6 DAY 1

READING COMPREHENSION:

1. Based on Paragraph I, Mr. Verloc's store is not usually very busy during the daytime, and he doesn't actually seem to care much about the actual health of the business. Additionally, he knows his wife will keep a close eye on the brother-in-law.

2. Answers will vary. Students should identify that the setting is somewhat "grimy," and that the store sells a seemingly random collection of mostly useless objects. The store also contains a loud bell that rings every time someone enters or exits.

3. C – "The shop was small" is one complete sentence. "So was the house" is another complete sentence. They are joined by a comma and the conjunction "and" because the two ideas reinforce or support each other.

4. B - All of the men seem very suspicious, since they dress in long coats that are pulled up to obscure their faces and always walk around with their hands in their pockets. We have no way of knowing for sure that they are spies, but they are definitely highly strange and suspicious.

5. Answers will vary. Based on the title and the descriptions of the other characters, students will probably predict that Mr. Verloc gets involved in some kind of spying or investigative scenario.

ENGLISH/GRAMMAR ACTIVITY:

1. A comma should be inserted after "merging this winter."

2. A comma should be inserted after "for fifteen years." Another comma should be added after "that time."

3. A comma should be inserted after "Piper" and a second (optional) comma can be inserted after "Allie." There should also be a comma inserted after "for the play."

4. A comma should be inserted after "read a comic book." A comma should also be inserted after "heroes," and an optional comma can be added after "villains."

5. A comma should be inserted after "Most days." A comma should be inserted after "in the cafeteria." A final comma should be inserted after "on my work."

WEEK 6 DAY 2
READING COMPREHENSION:

1. Answers will vary. Based on Paragraph 1, Mr. Verloc is observant and, within this passage, seems optimistic about things in general. He seems to be particular about his appearance, as his shoes are shined and his face is freshly shaven. The final paragraph shows that Mr. Verloc has a strong sense of responsibility and sees himself as a protector of the people.

2. Answers will vary. The description of the setting shows that things are unusually sunny for London, and that it appears to be a beautiful morning. The sun reflects off all the buildings brightly, and nothing seems to have a shadow. There are also wealthy people walking around or riding in carriages.

3. A - Paragraph 3 reveals that it is "a peculiarly London sun" that is creating all the golden light in the area. There is no literal gold in the passage at all; the term "gold" is only used to describe the color and beauty of the sunlight.

4. B - The final paragraph of the passage shows that Mr. Verloc believes he is protecting "the whole social order favourable to their hygienic idleness," meaning that part of his job is to make sure that rich people stay rich. He also reveals that the rich think of work (labour) as "unhygienic," meaning that they are lazy and look down on hard-working people, in his opinion.

5. Answers will vary. The final paragraph and a half of the passage reveal that Mr. Verloc sees all of society as something that needs to be protected. He doesn't just see things for what they are; he recognizes the long, complex back story behind everything. For example, when he sees people walking in the park with their carriages trailing behind them, he doesn't just see rich people walking; he sees the privileges of wealth and safety that people in London have.

ENGLISH/GRAMMAR ACTIVITY:

1. BUT is the appropriate conjunction. The new sentence should read, "Poisonous snakes can be highly dangerous for hikers, but there aren't any in this part of the state." (Some slight variation may occur.)

2. OR is the appropriate conjunction. The new sentence should read, "You can write your answers on the math test in the form of fractions or percentages." (Some slight variation may occur.)

3. AND is the appropriate conjunction. The new sentence should read, "There is going to be a demolition derby at the town fair, and everybody is excited to see the crazy spectacle."

WEEK 6 DAY 3

Real world problems multiply/divide fractions

1. D

2. $\frac{21}{12}$ or $1\frac{9}{12}$ of a mile

3. C

4. C

5. D

6. D

7. $7\frac{1}{8}$ hours

8. 88 pounds

9. C

10. B

11. $20\frac{4}{9}$

WEEK 6 DAY 4

Rounding numbers to thousands, hundreds, tens, ones, tenths, hundredths and thousandths place

1. C

2. B

3. C

4. B

5. A

6. D

7. C

8. B

9. C

10. C

11. B

12. C

13. 240

14. to the nearest thousand

15. 8.4

16. to the hundredths

17. 65.876

18. 8,000

19. 7.35 > 7.34

20. 7

WEEK 6 DAY 5

Area & Perimeter

1. A

2. C

3. B

4. A

ANSWER SHEET

5. C

6. D

7. D

8. C

9. B

10. Area is $1\frac{1}{4}$ sq ft,

perimeter is $4\frac{5}{6}$ ft

11. B

WEEK 6 DAY 6
Answers will vary.

WEEK 7 🌑 DAY 1
READING COMPREHENSION:

1. The thing is a working scale model of a time machine. The Time Traveller explicitly explains this in Paragraph 3.

2. The concept of time travel is generally considered to be impossible or fictional. The Time Traveller has invited reputable people to see his model and hear him explain his thinking so that people will not think he is insane.

3. C – "...the bright light of which fell upon the model" is nonessential or bonus information about the "small shaded lamp." Bonus information at the end of a sentence should be separated with a comma.

4. C – "This little affair" is the model of the time machine, as described in Paragraph 3. In this context, the Time Traveller is using the word to mean "this project" or "this gizmo."

5. Answers will vary. Students might suggest that many of the characters are named by their professions because they are not terribly important to the rest of the story. Others might suggest that this meeting is of a somewhat secret or "under cover" nature, so the people's identities have been protected.

ENGLISH/GRAMMAR ACTIVITY:

1. The sentence should read: "Our class president, Jackson Quarry, is also the captain of the boys' soccer team." The class president's specific name is bonus information in this context.

2. The sentence should read: "Michael forgot his sister's birthday again this year, which was a surprise to absolutely nobody." The fact that Michael consistently forgets his sister's birthday (or is generally absentminded) is bonus information about his character for the reader.

3. The sentence should read: "Francesca has been collecting sneakers since she was in the fourth grade, when she got her first pair of Air Jordans." The final phrase of the sentence provides bonus information, which explains what specific or special event occurred when Francesca was in the fourth grade.

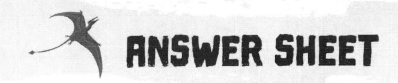

4. The sentence should read: "My wife's grandmother, who is the best cook I know, hosts an incredible holiday party every year." The fact that the speaker's wife's grandmother is a great cook is bonus information, as the main idea of the overall sentence is that she throws great holiday parties.

5. The sentence should read: "All the players on both teams took a knee as the injured player, who was a member of the Oakdale Lions, was tended to by a medic." The specific team affiliation of the injured player is bonus information in the sentence.

WEEK 7 ⚫ DAY 2

READING COMPREHENSION:

1. Answers may slightly vary. The Time Traveller is trying to prove to the others that his model time machine is not "trickery" or some sort of prank/hoax. Therefore, having somebody else operate the machine lends more credibility to the device than if he simply used it himself.

2. According to the sentence, the Psychologist is trying to act cool, calm, and collected, as if he was not disturbed by the tiny time machine. However, he attempts to light a cigar before it has been properly prepared, which shows that he is distracted and pre-occupied by thinking about the time machine.

3. B – "For certain" is a nonessential modifier because, if it were removed from the sentence, "I don't know which" would still carry the exact same meaning. This shows that it is simply bonus (extra) or nonessential information.

4. D – When the Medical Man asks "Are you in earnest about this?" he then follows by adding "Do you seriously believe that that machine has travelled in time?" This reveals that he is asking the Time Traveller weather he really believes what he is saying.

5. The Psychologist reasons that, if the machine travelled in time without moving, it must have gone to the past because it is no longer in the room. If the machine travelled to the future, he reasons, it would not disappear, but simply stay in the room between that moment and wherever it had gone in the future.

ENGLISH/GRAMMAR ACTIVITY:

1. The sentence should read: "At the grocery store, we picked up apples, tomatoes, and a jar of pickles." (The first comma separates the intro from the body of the sentence. The rest of the commas form a list.)

2. The sentence should read: "My favorite class is French because Monsieur Francois, who is actually from France, is an excellent teacher, and many other students agree with me." (The first two commas separate out the nonessential modifier "who is actually from France," while the final comma forms a compound sentence.)

ANSWER SHEET

3. The sentence should read: "After the earthquake, we had to sweep up some shards of shattered glass, fragments of decorative plates, and dirt from a potted plant, which had fallen from a shelf." (The first comma separates the intro from the body of the sentence. The next two commas form a list. The final comma separates the nonessential modifier "which had fallen from a shelf" from the main body of the sentence.)

4. The sentence should read: "I burned my hand on a radiator when I was young, so I am always extra careful around heaters, fireplaces, and stoves, especially in the winter." (The first comma creates a compound sentence using the subordinating conjunction "so." The next two commas are used to create a list. The final comma separates the nonessential modifier "especially in the winter" from the main body of the sentence.)

5. That old tree needs to have several branches trimmed, or it could create a dangerous situation in the winter, when the trees become heavy with snow. (The first comma creates a compound sentence. The second comma separates the nonessential modifier "when the trees become heavy with snow" from the main body of the sentence.)

WEEK 7 DAY 3

Writing algebraic expressions

1. A
2. D
3. B
4. D
5. C
6. B
7. B
8. C
9. C
10. A
11. $26 - M$
12. $15 \times C$
13. $D + 8$
14. $Y \times 36$
15. C
16. B
17. C
18. $16 \div Y$
19. $X \times 5$
20. $28 - F$

WEEK 7 DAY 4

Evaluating expressions

1. 39
2. C
3. D
4. B
5. 108
6. A
7. C
8. 132 sq in
9. C
10. C
11. B
12. $V = \frac{8}{27}$ in³, $A = \frac{8}{3}$ in²
13. 36 cm³
14. 81
15.
   A. 33
   B. 116
   C. 228
   D. 152
16. $V = 729$ cm³, $A = 486$ cm²
17. -76
18. $\frac{1}{3}$ sq in

237

ANSWER SHEET

WEEK 7 DAY 5

Generating equivalent expressions

1. C
2. D
3. B
4. A
5. C
6. B

7. B
8. C
9. D
10. C
11. $2x + y^2$
12. $18x + 60y$
13. $6(7x + 3y)$ or $3(14x + 6y)$
14. $2x - 6x^2$

15. $6x + 10y - 14$
16. $x + 10y$
17. $xy - y + 7$
18. $6x^2 - 3x$
19. $72x - 2y$
20. $25x^2 + 20x$

WEEK 7 DAY 6

Answers will vary.

WEEK 8 DAY 1

READING COMPREHENSION:

1. Answers may vary slightly. Long John is a smart, strong-willed, brave, and respected person, who people consider very mentally strong, but he is dealing with some form of disability that requires him to walk with a crutch and sometimes use ropes for support.

2. Answers may vary slightly. Long John appears to be friendly to Jim Hawkins, as he invites him to chat and shows him his talking parrot. Jim Hawkins, the narrator, seems to be somewhat fixated on Long John, as he talks to other crew members around him and studies the way he movies around the ship and works closely.

3. C - The passage never specifically says if Long John is missing a limb or has an artificial limb, but it does make it clear that he walks using a crutch and has some challenges when it comes to standing, balancing, and walking across the ship's deck when the sea is rough. However, he does not always use his crutch to walk, and instead sometimes uses ropes that are rigged up instead.

4. A - Jim Hawkins describes the parrot as squawking "Pieces of eight!"... with great rapidity," which suggests that it was very annoying. When Long John covers the cage during these outbursts, the reader can infer that his goal is to make the parrot be quiet.

5. Answers will vary. Students will probably predict that Long John and Jim Hawkins go on some kind of an adventure together.

ENGLISH/GRAMMAR ACTIVITY:

1. Fox is concrete. Dog is concrete.
2. Spaghetti is concrete. Meatballs are concrete. Plan is abstract.
3. Textbook is concrete. Understanding is abstract. Culture is abstract.
4. Object is abstract. Bowling is concrete. Pins are concrete.

ANSWER SHEET

WEEK 8 DAY 2

READING COMPREHENSION:

1. Based on the first paragraph, Jim believes that the crew are given more food and drink than is necessary. Anytime there is a birthday or any excuse for a special occasion or celebration, extra apples and grog are passed out.

2. Based on the final paragraph, Jim is looking for an apple to eat, and the barrel is quite empty. Attempting to find one final apple, he climbs into the barrel to look for it. He gets comfortable in the barrel and begins to doze off when somebody (Long John) sits up against it.

3. C - The way that Jim says he is "not allowed" to be more plain suggests he knows more than he is saying but cannot share it with the reader. Given the title, "Treasure Island," it's reasonable to assume that some people may have wanted to keep the island's location a secret.

4. B - When Jim says "...as you shall hear," he is specifically telling the reader that what he heard in the apple barrel is crucial to events later in the story. This is an example of foreshadowing.

5. Answers will vary. Based on the final sentences of the passage, students may predict that Jim overhears that Long John is part of some kind of bad or evil plot.

ENGLISH/GRAMMAR ACTIVITY:

1. Myth is abstract. George Washington is concrete. Tree is concrete.
2. Writer is concrete. Imagination is abstract. Confidence is abstract.
3. Pitcher is concrete. Focus is abstract. Baserunner is concrete.
4. Food is concrete. Airplanes are concrete. Quality is abstract.
5. Puppy is concrete. Floor is concrete. Enthusiasm is abstract.

WEEK 8 DAY 3

Converting measurements

1. C
2. D
3. C
4. C
5. D
6. B
7. A
8. C
9. B
10. B
11. C
12. 20 oz
13. 1,550 m
14. C
15. 3.022 km
16. 7:50 p.m.
17. 125,000 mm
18. 21 lbs 8 oz or $21\frac{1}{2}$ lbs

ANSWER SHEET

WEEK 8 DAY 4

Line plot to display data

1. C
2. D
3. B
4. B
5. C
6. D
7. D
8. C

9. B
10. D
11. B
12. 10

WEEK 8 DAY 5

Volume

1. C
2. B
3. D
4. C

5. A
6. C
7. B
8. D
9. C
10. A

WEEK 8 DAY 6

Answers will vary.

WEEK 9 DAY 1

READING COMPREHENSION:

1. Answers will vary slightly. Buck lives on a large, sunny property in the Santa Clara Valley (which students should be able to infer is in California). Buck appears to live on some kind of working farm, vineyard, or ranch, as there is extensive mention of vines, grapes, orchards, and a large number of servants.

2. Buck moves around the property where he lives however he wants. He is never confined in a kennel or forced to stay indoors. His day-to-day life is largely independent, unlike other dogs who are trapped or held in certain areas.

3. D – Based on Paragraph 1, the reader should be able to identify that many people are headed up to the "Northland" and that they need as many strong dogs as possible. "Trouble is brewing" because many dogs may have to leave their live as pets to go do hard work far away.

4. C – Based on context clues, students should be able to determine that "this great demesne" means "this very large property." All the descriptive details of Paragraph 2 suggest that a "demesne" is a large estate, and the phrase "...and here had had lived..." in Paragraph 3 communicates that a "demesne" is a certain kind of place.

5. Answers will vary. The author writes the passage as though Buck were the owner of the property. He is treated as the most important character, and many insights (about the strangeness of small dogs and the activities of servants) seem to be filtered through his point of view, almost as though he were a human, looking at the world around him.

ANSWER SHEET

ENGLISH/GRAMMAR ACTIVITY:

1. "Clean your room!" my mom shouted from downstairs.

2. Mr. Shapiro rolled his eyes and said, "I guess we're going to need to buy new towels."

3. "I am not a good dancer at all," Michelle said with a frown, "and I don't want to embarrass myself."

4. According to Einstein, "Anyone who has never made a mistake has never tried anything new."

5. "What's all that racket down there?" Mrs. Trowley called from upstairs. "I'm trying to get some sleep!"

WEEK 9 DAY 2

READING COMPREHENSION:

1. The passage reveals that Manuel is dishonest and basically kidnaps/steals Buck. The first paragraph reveals that Manuel is a gambler who is not good at handling money or taking care of his family.

2. Answers will vary slightly. When the Judge's family are all away from home, Manuel steals Buck and sells him to a man at a train station. Manuel also wraps a rope around Buck's neck to make him easier to control.

3. A - The tone of the conversation between Manuel and the stranger is dark and threatening because they don't seem to have any regard for Buck's safety or any sense of shame about what they are doing. They refer to putting a rope around Buck's neck as "wrap[ping] the goods," and they seem willing to choke Buck as a way to control him.

4. D - Buck growls at the precise moment that Manuel hands the rope to the stranger. According to the final paragraph, Buck growls to "intimate his displeasure," meaning that he wants to show that he doesn't like being given to a stranger.

5. Answers will vary. Based on this passage and the Day 1 passage, students should be able to predict that Buck may be going to the Northland to work.

ENGLISH/GRAMMAR ACTIVITY:

Teddy and Yosana walked out of the school building and looked up at the bright, blue sky.

"It's a beautiful day, Yosana marveled."

"Definitely," Teddy agreed. "it's so nice to be out of class for the day."

"I know! I almost hate to go home too fast," she agreed.

"Do you want to hang out at the park over by the library for a while?" Teddy suggested. "I have a flying disc in my backpack."

Yosana replied, "That sounds like fun, but I need to call my mom first to tell her where I'm going."

"That's a good idea," Teddy agreed. "I will text my parents as well."

Teddy and Yosana walked to the park, where they threw the flying disc back and forth for about an hour. Eventually, Yosana looked at her phone and noticed it was getting late.

"I have to be home by five," she explained, "because I have to make sure the dog goes for a walk before my parents get home."

"That's fine," Teddy said with a smile. "Let me walk you home."

Yosana smiled and said, "Thank you very much!"

WEEK 9 ⬤ DAY 3
Line of symmetry

1. Yes, it is.
2. D
3. B
4. B
5. D
6. B
7. C
8. D
9. No, it is not.
10.

WEEK 9 ⬤ DAY 4
Coordinate Plane

1. C
2. D
3. D
4. C
5. B
6. A
7. C
8. B
9. D
10. A
11. C
12. A
13. D
14. D
15. B

WEEK 9 ⬤ DAY 5
Classifying 2-d figures

1. B
2. A
3. D
4. B
5. A
6. A
7. parallelogram
8. trapezoid
9. C
10. D
11. A
12. D
13. B
14. C
15. D

WEEK 9 ⬤ DAY 6
Answers will vary.

ANSWER SHEET

WEEK 10 DAY 1

READING COMPREHENSION:

1. Answers will vary slightly. Based on the text of the poem, students should be able to infer that the story takes place very late at night indoors, in a "chamber" or room where the narrator is sitting alone. Students may also infer that the chamber is a library or study, many books are mentioned.

2. Based on Stanza 2, students should be able to infer that Lenore is a former girlfriend or close female acquaintance of the narrator and that she is probably dead.

3. B – Lines 2, 3, 4, 5, 16, 17, 21, and 22 all describe the sound of a knocking, tapping, rapping, etc. sound on the door.

4. C – The poem is written entirely in the past tense, and subject-verb agreement is only a major concern in the present tense.

5. Answers may vary slightly. Throughout the first three stanzas, the narrator is convinced someone is knocking at the chamber door. However, in Stanza 4, the door is opened, and nobody is there, which is unexpected and creepy.

ENGLISH/GRAMMAR ACTIVITY:

1. Incorrect. "Gets" should be changed to "get" because "Maurice and John" are a plural subject.

2. Incorrect. "Bandit are" should be changed to "Bandit is" because "Bandit" is a singular dog.

3. Incorrect. "Stand" should be changed to "stands" because "anyone" is a singular subject (which the word "one" should hint at).

4. Incorrect. "Eat" should be changed to "eats" because the "team" is a collective, which means it take singular verbs even though it represents a group of more than one person.

5. Correct. This sentence rewrites the sentence from Question 4 in a way that uses proper subject-verb agreement.

WEEK 10 DAY 2

READING COMPREHENSION:

1. Answers may vary slightly. At the end of Day 1's passage, the narrator opened his door (which he thought someone was knocking on) to reveal that nobody was there. He is all alone in the middle of the night, his mind is occupied thinking about someone he knew who is probably dead, and he keeps hearing strange sounds.

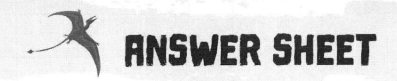

2. In the opening line of Stanza 3, the narrator opens the window ("flung the shutter"), allowing the bird to enter from the outside, where it had been tapping on the window.

3. D – At first, in Stanza 3, the narrator describes the Raven as a "stately Raven of the saintly days of yore." This is a very flattering description, as he makes the Raven sound regal and respectable. While it's true the Raven is later described as being grim or gloomy, the first description is actually positive.

4. C – At the end of Stanza 4, the narrator asks the Raven its name, and the Raven caws "Nevermore." The narrator interprets this to mean that the Raven's name is "Nevermore," which we can observe at the end of Stanza 5, when he describes the Raven as having "such name as 'Nevermore.'"

5. Answers will vary. Students may say that the raven is a dark bird, and the narrator is in a dark mood. It also appears that the raven really does want to communicate to the narrator, since it knocks repeatedly on the window, enters when the window is open, and seems to respond the narrator's questions. Students may also say that the word "Nevermore" may connect to the "lost Lenore" mentioned in Day One's passage.

ENGLISH/GRAMMAR ACTIVITY:

1. Answers will vary and are correct as long as the sentence makes sense and the verb is plural (to agree with the subject "We"). Plan, Take, Enjoy, Go on, etc. are all examples of good answers.

2. Answers will vary and are correct as long as the sentence makes sense and the noun is plural (to agree with the verb "swim"). Fish, Dolphins, Whales, Eels, Penguins, etc. are all examples of good answers.

3. Answers will vary and are correct as long as the sentence makes sense and the verbs are both singular (to agree with the subject "brother"). Tosses, Turns, Snores, Talks, Mumbles, Rolls over, etc. are all examples of good answers.

4. Answers will vary and are correct as long as the sentence makes sense and the noun is plural (to agree with the plural verb "tend"). Students, Kids, People, Learners, etc. are all examples of good answers.

5. Answers will vary and are correct as long as the sentence makes sense and the verb is singular (to agree with the singular subject "wind"). Blows, Howls, Breezes, Passes, Whispers, etc. are all examples of good answers.

ANSWER SHEET

WEEK 10 DAY 3
Solving and writing equations

1. D
2. C
3. B
4. A
5. D
6. C
7. A
8. C
9. $32x = 224$, $x = 7$
10. D
11. B
12. D
13. C
14. D
15. $y = 44$
16. $x = 7$

WEEK 10 DAY 4
Finding area of triangles

1. B
2. D
3. C
4. B
5. A
6. 64 sq cm
7. B
8. C
9. A
10. 88 sq in
11. 5 sq cm
12. $87\frac{1}{2}$ sq yd

WEEK 10 DAY 6
Answers will vary.

WEEK 10 DAY 5
Division

1. B
2. A
3. D
4. A
5. B
6. A
7. B
8. B
9. C
10. A
11. $1,638 \div 24 = 149$ r **6**
12. 47
13. 2,294
14. 78
15. C
16. 61
17. $5,933 \div 64 = 92$ r **45**
18. 243
19. 49
20. 64

ANSWER SHEET

WEEK 11 🌐 DAY 1

READING COMPREHENSION:

1. The castle is described as "ruined" in Paragraph 1, so students should understand that it has a rather rough and run-down appearance. Parts of the castle are decided as "broken," but the structure is still extremely large. The door is huge and old-fashioned.

2. Answers may vary slightly. The carriage driver is extremely strong, and he also abandons the narrator pretty much as soon as they arrive at the castle, rather than providing an explanation of what to do.

3. B - Throughout the passage, the narrator communicates that the castle has a dreamy feel. When he first arrives, he says, "I must have been asleep," and later describes that the castle "perhaps seemed bigger than it really is," which is also very dream-like. The strange behavior of the driver (and his sudden disappearance) both feel like something out of a dream. Towards the end of the passage, the narrator begins testing himself to double-check that he is awake and says, "It all seemed like a horrible nightmare to me, and I expected that I should suddenly awake."

4. A - In Paragraph 4, the narrator clearly states "I began to rub my eyes and pinch myself to see if I were awake."

5. Answers will vary. The setting contributes to the dark, ominous tone because the description of the castle itself as ruined and huge is rather eerie. The characters contribute to the dark/ominous tone, as the narrator has no idea what is going on, and the only other character, the driver, is strangely strong and disappears as quickly as possible. The plot contributes to the ominous tone as well, because the narrator is deeply scared but motivated to push forward because of his ambition to become a solicitor and impress Mina.

ENGLISH/GRAMMAR ACTIVITY:

1. The sentence is in the passive voice. You can tell because the subject (mailbox) is not the one who performed the verb (knocked over). In fact, it was the one getting knocked over.

2. The sentence is in the active voice. You can tell because the subject (dog) is the one performing the action of the main verb (pulled).

3. The sentence is in the passive voice. You can tell because the subject (area) is not the one "hitting" anything. Instead, it is being hit.

4. The sentence is in the active voice. You can tell because the subject (us - contained in the contraction "Let's") is the one performing the actions described (building and studying).

5. The sentence is in the passive voice. You can tell because the subject (nails) is getting bitten rather than biting anyone.

ANSWER SHEET

WEEK 11 DAY 2

READING COMPREHENSION:

1. Like the Day One passage, this section of the text has a somewhat ominous mood, as the castle is still a creepy visual, and the corpse-like appearance of Dracula is bizarre. However, unlike the last passage, this piece contains some almost humorous strangeness. Dracula's theatrical repetition of the line "Welcome to my house!" stands out as quirky, and his appearance, described in Paragraph 2, is also slightly comedic. At the end of the passage, the elderly Dracula offers to carry the younger narrator's luggage, which is also slightly strange and humorous.

2. Based on Paragraph 2, the lamp that Dracula carries does not have any sort of shade or chimney on it, so its flame keeps dancing around randomly, casting strange shadows and creating constant fluctuations between areas of light and darkness. This visual contributes to the overall creepy mood.

3. C - When the narrator shakes Dracula's hand in Paragraph 4, he notices that Dracula is very strong and immediately compares it to the handshake of the driver. In fact, the narrator pauses for a minute to wonder if they two characters are actually the same person.

4. D - Dracula's pale skin is mentioned earlier in the passage, but it is only when the narrator shakes his hand in Paragraph 3 that he discovers that Dracula is "as cold as ice - more like the hand of a dead than a living man."

5. Answers will vary. Dracula has a rather creepy appearance and manner, but he is also extremely hospitable to the narrator and genuinely seems to want to welcome and impress him. He also seems to have a quirky, grandiose way of talking.

ENGLISH/GRAMMAR ACTIVITY:

1. Answers will vary slightly. "A careful, cunning spider wove the massive web in the corner of our kitchen" would be an example of a concise, correct answer.

2. Answers will vary slightly. "A professional football team in Texas picked my cousin Corey in the third round of the draft" would be an example of a concise, correct answer.

3. Answers will vary slightly. "Many Americans consider the United States Postal Service to be one of the most important services in our country" is an example of a concise, correct answer.

4. Answers will vary slightly. "Early yesterday morning, a thief stole my car while I was sleeping" is an example of a concise, correct answer.

5. Answers will vary slightly. "Juan Cabrera hit that home run so hard that, if it wasn't for the scoreboard, it would've gone out of the stadium" is an example of a concisce, correct answer.

ANSWER SHEET

WEEK 11 DAY 3

Ratios and rates

1. D
2. C
3. B
4. C
5. B
6. B
7. B
8. 5 : 37
9. 8 : 7
10. 63
11. B
12. $8
13. D
14. 35
15. $6
16. D
17. 20 oz
18. C

WEEK 11 DAY 4

Angles (Right Angles, Acute Angles, Obtuse Angles) and finding angles of shapes

1. It is less than a right angle.

2.

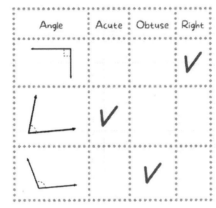

Angle	Acute	Obtuse	Right
			✓
	✓		
		✓	

3.
   A. Acute
   B. Right
   C. Acute
   D. Obtuse

4.
   Number of acute angles - 1
   Number of obtuse angles - 3
   Number of right angles - 1

5. C

6.
   10° - Acute
   110° - Obtuse
   45° - Acute
   135° - Obtuse

7. C
8. 6
9. 9
10. 2

WEEK 11 DAY 5

Greatest Common Factor/ Least Common Multiple

1. C
2. D
3. B
4. B
5. D
6. B
7. C
8. D
9. C
10. D
11. B
12. C
13. C
14. B
15. D
16. 28
17. B
18. 3
19. 4
20. A

WEEK 11 DAY 6

Answers will vary.

ANSWER SHEET

WEEK 12 DAY 1

READING COMPREHENSION:

1. Answers may vary. Dr. Jekyll is a friendly, handsome man. However, his generally friendly and warm manner changes when Mr. Hyde and his will are mentioned, and he seems very distracted, frustrated, and dismayed.

2. Mr. Utterson is a loyal and devoted friend who wants to ensure that Dr. Jekyll is safe from fear or threats. He considers himself a trustworthy person and desperately wants to help others.

3. D – In Paragraph 1, the narrator establishes that Mr. Utterson frequently stays after larger parties to have quieter, more personal conversations with people. In Paragraph 2, Utterson specifically explains that he has stayed behind in hopes of talking to Jekyll about the recent changes to his will.

4. A – Dr. Jekyll's response to mention of Hyde is various mysterious because he seems to display several different emotions at once. He seems both annoyed and a little defensively angry, while also attempting to smooth things out and reassure Utterson. Overall, he displays very strange behavior that suggests that something is wrong, in spite of his objections.

5. Answers will vary. Utterson may be concerned that Mr. Hyde has somehow threatened Dr. Jekyll into leaving him money and properly. He has heard negative things about Hyde, so he wants to be sure that Jekyll included him in his will of his own free will.

ENGLISH/GRAMMAR ACTIVITY:

1. Opinion. "Most beautiful" should have been a major hint (judgmental language).

2. Fact. "Average" and "27 degrees Fahrenheit" should have been indicators (evidence/support/statistics)

3. Opinion. The first part of the sentence ("The Country Café is popular") could be an objective fact, but "nobody likes the pancakes" is an oversimplification, which demonstrates that it's an opinion.

4. Fact. "Statistics show" should have been a major indicator (evidence/support/statistics)

5. Opinion. "More important" should have been an indicator to the reader, as it shows a value judgment that someone could easily disagree with without being wrong.

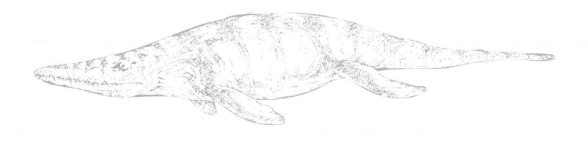

ANSWER SHEET

WEEK 12 DAY 2

READING COMPREHENSION:

1. At the beginning of the story about the maid, she appears to be having a wonderful night and is enjoying the beauty of the full moon while feeling "more at peace" than ever before. However, the rest of the passage contrasts sharply to that feeling, as it describes a very violent and traumatic physical attack.

2. Even before he attacks the old man, Mr. Hyde seems to have a very evil or mean personality, according to the maid. She explains that "she had conceived a dislike" for him during previous experiences, and before he attacks the man, his body language seems extremely hostile and mean.

3. B – In Paragraphs 2-3, the maid describes the old man as very polite, respectful, kind, and even "beautiful."

4. A – The opening sentences of Paragraph 4 reveal that Mr. Hyde's anger and the quickness with which it escalates are extremely disturbing to the young maid.

5. Answers may vary slightly. In Day One's passage, Dr. Utterson expressed concern that Mr. Hyde was a bad, potentially dangerous person. In this passage, we see confirmation that Hyde is indeed a very bad, hurtful person.

ENGLISH/GRAMMAR ACTIVITY:

1. Fact. "Competitive" should be an indicator because the speaker does not claim to be "the best" or "the greatest," but instead simply states what the office provides.

2. Opinion "Great place" should have been a major indicator that someone was expressing personal opinion (since it could be reasonably disagreed with). Additionally, "everyone here thinks of the team is a family" should be a hint because it's possible that many employees might not think an environment like that was "great."

3. Opinion. "Not as exciting" is clearly a statement of personal preference rather than fact. Furthermore, some people might actually enjoy that you "focus on the same two players for a long time."

4. Fact. "Most people" is general enough without oversimplifying things, and the sentence avoids making any overly dramatic claims.

5. Opinion. Someone could reasonably agree with the first part of the sentence without being wrong. Saying lemons are "perfect" should've been a major indicator.

ANSWER SHEET

WEEK 12 DAY 3

End of Summer Assessment (Mixed Questions)

1. 512
2. $ 38.65
3. $15\frac{3}{16}$
4. $25\frac{7}{8}$
5. 9
6. $\frac{9}{63}$ or $\frac{1}{7}$
7. 7
8. D
9. C
10. B
11. D
12. $\frac{3}{15}, \frac{11}{20}, \frac{8}{12}, \frac{5}{6}$
13. $\frac{27}{24}$ or $1\frac{1}{8}$
14. B
15. D

WEEK 12 DAY 4

End of Summer Assessment (Mixed Questions)

1. 24 sq in
2. B
3. 4
4. 14 ft
5. 3,456 cubic feet
6.

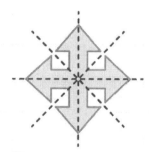

7. 7
8. B
9. A
10. D
11. Yes, it is.
12. C
13. D
14. D

WEEK 12 DAY 5

End of Summer Assessment (Mixed Questions)

1. A
2. 2(23-14)
3. 1,030,111
4. B
5. A
6. 56,128 - **33,979** = 22,149
7. D
8. B
9. A
10. C
11. 32
12. 5
13. B
14. C
15. D
16. B
17. 5,769
18. C
19. 4, 11, 20, 31, **44**, 59, 76
20.

Input (x)	6	8	14	32	57	63
Output (y)	21	23	29	47	**72**	78

WEEK 12 DAY 6

Answers will vary.

ANSWER SHEET

WEEK 1 DAY 7

WEEK 2 DAY 7

1 - E
2 - C
3 - D
4 - B
5 - A
6 - H
7 - G
8 - F

WEEK 3 DAY 7

1 - D
6 - A
3 - F
2 - B
4 - E
5 - C

WEEK 4 DAY 7

WEEK 5 DAY 7

1 - 3
2 - 6
4 - 8
5 - 7

WEEK 6 DAY 7

Headphones #2

WEEK 7 DAY 7

ANSWER SHEET

WEEK 8 DAY 7

DOWN:
1 - Wisp
2 - Shaver
3 - Toothpaste
4 - Hairdryer
5 - Hairbrush
6 - Shampoo
7 - Bathrobe

ACROSS:
6 - Spray
8 - Brush
9 - Mirror
10 - Soap
11 - Toothbrush
12 - Towel

WEEK 9 DAY 7

1 - A
2 - E
3 - D
4 - B
5 - C

WEEK 10 DAY 7

Answers will vary.

WEEK 11 DAY 7

A - 11
B - 5
C - 3
D - 9
E - 13

WEEK 12 DAY 6

1 - 2
4 - 7
5 - 3
8 - 6

Made in the USA
Middletown, DE
19 March 2020